Total Tripping

Total Tripping

CANADA

CARL LAHSER

 www.trafford.com

North America & international
toll-free: 1 888 232 4444 (USA & Canada)
fax: 812 355 4082

Contents

Contents

Where Have All the Pretty Colored Houses Gone?

An Objective View of Changes in Newfoundland 1961 to 2003

Carl Lahser

Contents

Where Have All the Pretty Colored Houses Gone?

Introduction. I retired from the US Air Force in January of 2003. At the time I had over forty years in natural resources such as pest management, grounds maintenance, bird strike prevention, and urban forestry. Checking frequent flyer miles I had accumulated I found I had about 10 trips on five airlines that had to be used by 2006.

I had been stationed at Argentia, Newfoundland, so for one trip maybe I could revisit Newfoundland? My wife said, "Go", so I did. I always take notes and write a "trip report". The report on Nova Scotia and Newfoundland follows.

In the beginning. I was in the barracks on Pensacola Naval Air Station in Pensacola, Florida, during March of 1960 when one of the guys said I had orders for Argentia. Wow! I didn't know the Navy had anything in South America so I hurried over to the personnel office.

My orders were actually to Naval Air Station Argentia, Newfoundland. I asked where Argentia was and somebody thought it was off the Atlantic coast of Canada. I also had orders for a six-week school in Willie Victor systems at Patuxant River Naval Air Station in Maryland on the way to Argentia.

I was an aviation electronics technician and had been in the Navy a little over a year. I had only been out of Texas twice. I had no idea what a Willie Victor was or where Maryland was much less Argentia. An evening in the base library helped a lot. The encyclopedia showed me where Maryland and Newfoundland were but not much detail. There was nothing about either specific place. I learned that the Willie Victor was an early warning radar version of the three-tailed commercial airliner called the Constellation. The Navy called it the WV2 Warning Star.

The first trip. A shipmate and I drove my car home to San Antonio, Texas, for two weeks leave. Then we drove across Louisiana, Mississippi, Alabama and Georgia to Naval Air Station at Brunswick, Georgia, where I dropped him off. I got on US highway 1 and drove north through Savannah, across the Carolinas and Virginia to Patuxant River southeast of Washington, D.C.

The school was a cram course in operation and repair of the APS-20 search radar, the APS-45 height finder radar, ECM equipment, radar consoles, and the other electronic and electrical equipment on the plane. I still learned almost nothing about what I would be doing at Argentia. The American Automobile Association provided a map of how to get to Argentia by road and ferry.

In mid-May I was back on US 1 for a ten-day drive to Argentia-Baltimore, Philadelphia, Newark, New York City, Boston, up through Maine to Calais. I crossed into New Brunswick and drove along the coast to Saint John and the reversing falls, then inland to Moncton. I crossed into Nova Scotia near Amherst and drove onward to Truro, New Glasgow, Antigonish, and Mulgrave to North Sydney and the ferry to Port-aux-Basque. I remember passing the tidal bore near Truro and the Reversing Falls near Saint John. The provinces were called the Maritime Provinces.

The ferry left in the evening and arrived at Port-aux-Basques as the sun was rising. I was really impressed with the colored houses along the green flat top coast—red, yellow, green and blue.

I drove off the ferry and headed for Argentia along the Trans-Canada Highway. After a couple miles I was surprised when the highway changed into a dirt road. Someone forgot to mention that only a few miles of black top were available in all of Newfoundland. Dirt road changed to single lane in places and forded creeks instead of crossing bridges. I was told later that the road was not really open for traffic yet from the spring thaw. This was late May.

It was supposed to take about 18 hours to drive from Port-aux-Basque to St Johns. After 14 hours of driving I was a little over half way there.

I dozed off near Glenwood and ran off the road. A logging truck driver helped me back on the road. I continued on a few miles and stopped for the rest of the night under red wool blankets at the Canadian Air Force Base at Gander. Next morning I got directions and arrived at Argentia in mid-afternoon.

I remember dirt road, lots of rocks, almost no traffic, stunted forest, numerous small villages, several fantastic seascapes, and a lot of good people but all this was over 40 years ago.

Argentia 1960. As an impressionable 22 year-old E-4 for my first 90 days on base I was assigned to the base police. This was very educational and beat the Dickens out of being assigned to the mess hall or barracks Master-at-Arms force. I got to know the base and a number of Bosons Mates and Gunners Mates, the tugboat crews and many Marines that I would probably not have met otherwise. We worked 24 hours then had 48 hours off. One of the guys had a girl friend so we would trade shifts and work 48 hours on to get fives days off. I spent much of this time off at a cabin at Placentia Junction on the railroad seven miles from the closest road. Details I remember about staying at the cabin include fresh trout for breakfast cooked on a wood stove and the English soap opera called Crabtree Corners.

After the base police I was assigned to the electronics shop and to an aircrew. We worked five days on and changed the shift every week. My crew had training classes and flew a 12-14 hour flight about twice a week. We stopped over night Lajas Air Base in the Azores about once a month for standby incase of bad weather at Argentia. When the BMEWS radar came on-line we began flying deployments to Keflavik Air Base, Iceland, just before I left in the fall of 1961.

The pavement ended at the base's main gate. On weekends we drove about two hours of rough road into St Johns. We sometimes went to a dance hall at Collinet or Whitborne, or the bar over the water in Placentia. There was an abandoned silver mine on base that we found by accident. We fished in the water supply reservoir in the summer and fall and skated there in the winter. We caught Capelins (<u>Mallotus villosus</u>) along the beach in June in "Capelin weather" that marks the beginning of summer. We picked bakeapples (<u>Rubus chamaemorus</u>) and strawberries

(Fragaria sp.) in the summer and blueberries (Vaccinium angustifolium) and cranberries (Vaccinium vitis-idaea) in the fall.

I rented a 21-foot fishing boat with an old Atlantic 2-cycle engine for three months and jigged cod and dogfish sharks or looked at Minke whales.

I met Mike Nolan who was the gamekeeper on the Salmonier line and went fishing and hunting with him. The sealing fleet was still operating. Cod was plentiful to be jigged and dried.

Squid were jigged for bait and food. A new freezer plant had just been built in Holyrood that froze squid, tuna and blueberries.

But, again, this was over 40 years ago.

The Return Trip. Continental was only airline with which I had frequent flyer miles that came anywhere close to Newfoundland. I booked a flight to Halifax and reserved a rental car for 11 September. I had not been to Nova Scotia or Newfoundland since 1961 except for refueling stops at Gander or Goose Bay. Maps showed new roads and parks and there were a lot of places I had never visited. I planned a three-week tour with a return from Halifax on 5 October. Computer searches found a lot of information. I even booked rooms for the trip and received my e-ticket on the computer.

References included *Some Newfoundland Vernacular Plant Names* and *A Checklist of the Vascular Plants of the Province of Newfoundland* by Ernest Rouleau published in 1956, *The Plants of Prince Edward Island* by David Erskine, *Wild Flowers of Newfoundland* by Bill and June Titford, *Traveling with Wildflowers* by Phyllis Hammond, Richard Preston's *North American Trees*, *Plants of the Western Boreal Forest and Aspen Parkland* by Kershaw and Pojar, Peterson's *Field Guide to the Birds*, *Birds of Newfoundland* by Burleigh and Peters, bird checklists of Terra Nova National Park and the Codroy Valley, *The Butterflies of North America* by James Scott, *Marine Life of Terra Nova National Park*, Michael Collins' *Life on the Newfoundland Seashore*, and the *Compendium of Seashells* and *Compendium of Land Snails* by Abbott and Dance.

Day 1, 11 Sep 2003. September 11 finally arrived. On September 11, 2011 the terrorist had hit New York and Washington, and some people were afraid to fly on this date. My wife dropped me at the airport at 0700 for my 0855 flight. There were no passengers at the Continental counter so check-in was quick. I removed my film and took the bags to the x-ray machines. They checked the bags and i replaced the film. There was a single line into the metal detectors but there were three detectors so this went fast. I removed my shoes and ran them through the machine before going through the detector. They found my metal hip so I got a pat down. I was at the gate by 0720.

The sun tried to come up but was beaten down by the low clouds. This was Gulf moisture overrun by a front. The MD80 was off the ground five minutes early. We were out of the wet stuff shortly and could see high stratus clouds with a few thunderheads beginning to build. After a few bumps we arrived in Houston five minutes early.

The gate for the next flight was a half-mile walk then I read until boarding time. Then we sat on the taxiway for almost an hour waiting in a long line for the 777-200 to takeoff for this 2200 km leg to Newark. The air controllers had increased takeoff intervals to one minute instead of 30 seconds.

Some cumulus thunderheads were building. We passed the stratus layer at 18,000 feet heading SE to Ellington. We turned east along the Gulf then inland to Baton Rouge and north of Mobile passing over the cirrus layer at 33,000 feet. The pilot angled a little to the north to Montgomery, LaGrange, Winston Salem, east of Washington DC, over Annapolis, Wilmington and into Newark. There was a couple minutes of clear air turbulence over Washington. All the hot air from the new session of Congress, I guess.

We landed smoothly. At 1700 we began boarding the 727 for the 600 mile ride to Halifax and were off the ground on time. Take off was to the south with a turn to the north. There was a large port complex and several bridges. A blue-green Statue of Liberty stood out in the bay. Up the river was New York City with Central Park and lots of buildings.

Thirty years previously when I had flown into Philadelphia, you could not see the city through the brown cloud but could smell the pollution as soon as the plane depressurized. That was the week the city changed from high sulfur soft coal to a low sulfur hard coal and there was an immediate change in air quality. This time it was hazy but you could see New York City. I have wasted a lot of film shooting bad pictures of hazy cities.

We quickly climbed above the cloud layer, the remains of Hurricane Henri. The sun set with the eastern horizon a pink glow. This was the night after the Harvest moon and Mars was up and shining two hours ahead of the moon. After an hour the clouds disappeared. Dark masses of islands in the

Bay of Fundy appeared breaking up gray water reflecting the full moon. Soon there were scattered lights followed by the lights of Halifax/Dartmouth.

The new airport was about 25 km NW of town. Last time I was in Halifax the airport was literally downtown. Immigration and customs were nothing. I got my bags, picked up my rental car, a gray Chrysler Sebring, and headed for Halifax. There was a lot of black between the airport and town.

I found the general area of Dartmouth where the Block House Bed and Breakfast was located but it took a couple turns around the area to find the address. Almost everything was closed so no money exchange or supper.

The B&B had two rental rooms each with hardwood floors and maple colonial furnishings. A shared bath was down the hall. There was also a sitting room with TV and phone. The hosts provided tea and muffins. I wrote up my notes before crawling under the feather comforter.

So ends day one.

Day 2, 12 Sep 2003. I woke up several times from the three-hour time change and finally got up at 0600. Temp was 15°C or about 62°F. My bags needed to be reorganized to find things more easily. When this was finished I went down for breakfast about 0730. After breakfast I called every publisher in the yellow pages and found no one who did poetry or regional histories. They considered poetry as fiction and said they could not publish me anyway since I was not Canadian.

I left about 0930 to find a bank. The exchange rate was $1.433 Canadian for a US dollar. I wandered on down the hill to ferry landing to cross to Halifax. The senior fare was $1.25 each way. The ferry ran every half hour and took 20 minutes for the trip. Quiet water on a clear day. Navy ships. Freighters. Cruise ship. Large suspension bridge. Nice scenic ride.

Shops in several malls along the waterfront had all the tourist stuff. One shop of particular interest sold flower pictures with the real flowers, which they laminated in UV resistant plastic and mounted on a glass cover.

I went inland up Prince Street to Barrington Street and turned roughly south. Old buildings dating to the late 1800s were mixed with new high-rise office buildings. Young maples were just beginning to change color. Several antique shops and half a dozen bookstores were located along this street.

The sidewalks contained a path of bricks about two feet wide stretching between the streetlights for easy utility access. The streets were clean. No signs of homeless people although there were street artists, tarot readers and musicians.

Many of the power poles and lampposts were plastered with theatre bills advertising current club acts and other activities. Looked like an active arts community.

The tourist information center provided a map of the province and brochures on what to see along the coast.

Turning up Spring Garden Road I passed St. Paul's cemetery, the courthouse, DAL Technical school, and the public library. I reached Spring Garden Place mall but was disappointed by the lack of variety in the businesses.

Back along Barrington I found the art museum. They have a shop that sells and rents art works as well as a museum store. One exhibit was of Maud Lewis primitive art. There was also a collection of Inuit and native art, Halifax area art and works by Nova Scotian painters. I had lunch at the museum about 1400—a salmon crepe, tea and a piece of chocolate mousse torte that was almost good enough to eat.

Back at the waterfront I sat in the afternoon sun and watched the activity in the harbor and the gulls in the bay. Ring-bill and Herring Gulls rested on the water while pigeons and starlings patrolled the sidewalks.

Local vegetation included Linden trees (Tilia vulgaris) and Plane trees (Platanus occidentalis), maples mostly red (Acer rubrum), plantain (Plantago major), Prostrate Knotweed (Ploygonum aviculare), red clover (Trifolium pratense), white clover (Trifolium repens), Oxalis (Oxalis sp), Yarrow (Achillea millefolium), Goldenrod (Solidago puberula), Black Knapweed (Centaurea nigra) and Joe-Pye Weed (Eupatorium maculatum). There were several giant white hydrangea tall as a house that were tinged with pink from recent frosts. Casual observations indicated the urban forest was pretty much mature trees in the same age class. Streets, curbs and sidewalks had been installed requiring the tree roots being pruned and constraining the root ball. I also noticed the pruning for electrical line clearance was behind schedule.

I took the ferry back to Dartmouth at 1630, returned to my room and dozed in front of the TV.

Day 3, 13 Sep 2003. I was up about 0600 and packed up. Everything had been mixed to get two bags weighing no more than 50 lbs each.

I went down for breakfast at 0730. French toast and tea. We discussed President Bush's war budget and my poetry. I paid the bill, loaded the bags, visited the yard sale next door (thankfully I was not terribly tempted) and left headed for highway 4 down the coast. A roadkill porcupine was on the road shoulder.

The road went through the woods with occasional ponds many of which were coves off the Atlantic Ocean. There were lots of yard sales along the highway but mostly kids clothing. All of the Ostrich Fern (<u>Matteuccia</u> <u>struthiopteris</u>) along the road was frost-burned.

First stop was at Clam Harbor Park. From the parking lot the trail led through scrub hazel, maple and spruce mixed with purple aster, yellow daisy and goldenrod to the beach backed with Spartina. The mud beach was strewn with Bladder Wrack (<u>Fucus</u> <u>vesiculosus</u>) and other seaweed from rocky bottoms. There were shells of Rock Crabs (<u>Cancer</u> <u>irroratus</u>) and broken Soft Shelled Clam shells (<u>Mya</u> <u>arenaria</u>). A flock of Semipalmated Plovers (<u>Charadrius</u> <u>semipalmatus</u>) were feeding for the long migration flight.

I stopped at an antique store only to find it had wholesaled the inventory and gone out of business.

There were white butterflies, the Sharp-Veined White (<u>Pieris</u> <u>napi</u>), about an inch long with a black border over the spartina and other roadside vegetation.

As I crossed one of the bridges I saw a Bald Eagle (<u>Haliaeetus</u> <u>leucocephalus</u>) sitting on a sand bar. Three hen ring-necked pheasants (<u>Phasianus</u> <u>colchicus</u>) crossed the road and one flew into my car.

Other stops along the road to look at vegetation found Lupine (<u>Lupinus</u> <u>polyphylus</u>) leaves, Evening Primrose (<u>Oenothera</u> <u>parviflora</u>), a small clover, lots of raspberry plants (<u>Rubus</u> <u>Idaeus</u>) and Northeastern Rose (<u>Rosa</u> <u>nitida</u>).

Near Harrigan Cove I stopped to look at a rocky beach. Besides lots of Bladder Wrack (<u>Fucus</u> <u>fascicule's</u>) and Spiral Wrack (<u>Fucus</u> <u>spiralis</u>), there were dead shells of Blue Mussels (<u>Mytilus</u> <u>edulis</u>), soft clams (<u>Mya</u> <u>arenaria</u>) and Dogwhelk (<u>Thais lapillus</u>). I turned over a big piece of plywood and found a lot of black earwigs that quickly disappeared into the sand. Above high tide were dead plants that looked like pokeweed and very healthy Red Raspberry and Goldenrod (<u>Solidago</u> <u>sp.</u>) A Belted Kingfisher (<u>Megaceryle</u> <u>alcyon</u>) flew over.

Another roadkill, a poor old porcupine.

I stopped at Sherbrook for a break and directions. I decided to continue up highway 4 to Antigonish instead of going around to Ft. Louisbourg. The road ran inland across the peninsula through the woods much like the roads to Ft McMurray and around Lake Winnipeg except the roadway was only 30 meters wide instead of over the hundred meters to provide a fire break in Alberta.

About 20km out of Antigonis the soil changed and farming replaced the woods. Truck crops. Hay. Dairy. I stopped and bought some tomatoes, plums and apples.

I hooked up with the TCH in Antigonis and was in at my motel in Port Hastings on Cape Breton Island about 1800. The TCH crossed the Canso Causeway on a riprap dike except for the bridge across the Canso Canal. The canal appeared to be a man-made cut to link the Gulf of St. Lawrence to the head of the Strait of Canso and cutting Cape Breton off from the mainland.

The backyard of the motel looked over the Strait. Turf was a Bluegrass mixed with all the east coast spring weeds such as three kinds of clover, purple New York Aster (<u>Aster</u> <u>novae-belgii</u>), Selfheal (<u>Prunella</u> <u>vulgaris</u>), Yarrow, Crown Vetch (<u>Coronilla</u> <u>varia</u>).

Day 4, 14 Sep 2003. I walked around the backyard of the motel and found some raspberries and wild apple and crabapple trees. The raspberries were good but the apple and crabapple were small, mealy and tasteless. Several White-Throated Sparrows (<u>Zonotrichia</u> <u>albicollis</u>) and a Black-poll Warbler (<u>Dendroica</u> <u>striata</u>) played around in the fruit trees.

The day's road was Highway 19 north along St. Georges Bay then NNE along the Gulf of St. Lawrence. A stop at a day park found Bunchberry (<u>Cornus</u> <u>canidensis</u>) and a squirrel. Roadside ditches were filled with cattails (<u>Typha</u> <u>latifolia</u>).

I took the Shore Road and stopped along the beach road near Maryville. Soft clams, razor clams (<u>Ensis</u> <u>directus</u>), Blue Mussels and Smooth Periwinkles (<u>Littorina</u> <u>obtusata</u>) were found. The water was clear and the rocks were covered with small Northern Rock Barnacles (<u>Semibalanus</u> <u>balanoides</u>) and Common Periwinkles (<u>Littorina</u> <u>littorea</u>). Introduced alfalfa (<u>Medicago</u> <u>sativa</u>), butter-and-eggs (<u>Linaria</u> <u>vulgaris</u>), Queen Anne's Lace (<u>Daucas</u> <u>carota</u>), and Cow Vetch (<u>Vicia</u> <u>cracca</u>) grew along the roadside. There was a harvester ant mound at roadside.

Gas at Mabou was $0.84/liter. That's over $3.00 a gallon US.

A pair of young raccoons who had been hit lay in the highway.

A stop at Inverness Harbor found lots of crab and lobster pots and a beach of tan sand and mixed small stones of shale, granite, sandstone and conglomerate. There were few shells.

I stopped at a craft shop. The shop had nothing of particular interest but the Bluegrass turf had east coast spring weeds such as red clover, Common Chickweed (<u>Stellaria</u> <u>media</u>), Fall Dandelion (<u>Leontodon</u> <u>autmnalis</u>), plantain (<u>Plantago sp.</u>) and Pearly Everlasting (<u>Anaphalis</u> <u>margaritacea</u>).

I decided to go across to Baddeck then down the TCH to North Sydney instead of going around Cape Breton Highlands National Park. Individual red maples were bright red. A few oaks were scarlet. Aspen were bright yellow.

Baddeck was the retirement home of Alexander Graham Bell and became a tourist attraction.

In North Sydney I stopped at a gas station for directions and finally found the motel. I thought it was because of no business but Nova Scotia closed almost everything on Sunday. Only the gas station and two restaurants were open.

Day 5, 15 Sep 2003. I left the motel at 0300 for the ferry. It only took about 15 minutes to drive to the ferry gate. The fare was $182.75 Canadian with senior discount. I got in line with trucks, campers, and a bus to wait for loading. About 0430 the ferry docked and the vehicles off-loaded. At 0515 we began to drive on board. I parked and went to the lounge on deck 5. Since the trip was mostly in daylight I did not get a cabin or sleeper dorm. I used the 14-hour trip to socialize and see the sea.

We left at 0600 on the dot. The trip began with a safety briefing.

There was no sunrise. A fog bank on the eastern horizon turned pink and the sun appeared full grown about a hour up. There was a light breeze and a long, low swell and a light chop sculpted the sea. The sea was a dark gray-green with clumps of seaweed. The smoke plume of a tanker in the distance bent horizontal showing a low inversion layer.

There were few birds on the trip. A few gulls. A Sooty Shearwater (<u>Puffinus griseus).</u> Small groups of Leach's Petrel (<u>Oceanodroma</u>

leucorhoa) that swam or flew weakly. Gannets (Morus bassanus) began to appear as we approached St. Pierre.

Sea Pigeons

Tiptoeing on the surface
On the trough between the waves
Scaring up fish

* * *

I saw two Humpback Whales. One was sounding with a wave of the tail and one broached near the ship. The distinctive spray pattern of five Finned Whales appeared. Several Minke or Pothead Whales broached in the distance. We also passed a small pod of White Beaked Porpoise that broached individually and then all seven jumped at once.

A tanker and several trawlers passed in the distance. We passed floats of crab traps on the banks. Smaller coastal fishing boats appeared as we approached St Pierre. We were in French territorial water, and we passed close to St Pierre about 1500.

About 1600 hills of the Avalon Peninsula appeared. We docked about 2030. A chop appeared about an hour before docking as we neared the harbor. Locals call this the Argentia tide.

Somehow I missed the tourist information office on the way to Placentia. It took several stops with roughly the same instructions to find the Harold Hotel. It was "down the road a piece on the Main road". If this looks like it lacks a frame of reference you are correct. I checked in and got a Bluestar beer and crashed.

Day 6, 16 Sep 2003. I worked on the computer and finally left at 0900. I found the Visitor Information office. It had displays of the history of the military at Argentia. The attendant was moderately helpful by providing a map of the new Argentia Backland Park but there were no maps of the old base.

I drove around the old base property and found most of the buildings gone and the sites being remediated. Even the Miami hangar and the barracks were gone and the runways abandoned. Lots of digging and rock hauling. There was a sign commemorating the Marine barracks. The ferry dock and a separate commercial dock facility in operation and a copper smelting facility was being built to refine copper ore from Labrador.

My first Backland walk was to Argentia Pond that once provided water for the base. I had camped out there one night in October and it was cold enough to freeze my canteen solid. The road was through Spruce trees and lined with many of the introduced weeds. The trail intersected another trail to a couple overlooks. Moss (Selaginella Selaginoides) covered the ground. Bunchberries or Crackerberry, creeping snowberry (Gaultheria hispidula), Chrysanthemum (Chrysanthemum leucanthemum), Mouse-Ear Chickweed (Cerastium vulgatum), a few Shrubby Cinquefoil (Potentilla fruticosa), strawberry (Fragaria virginiana) and Small Flowered Evening Primrose (Oenothera parviflora) and Common Anemones (Ranunculus acris), goldenrod grew along the trail. The gray-green lichen, Powdery Beard (Usnea sp.), hung from the branches like Spanish moss. Gray crustose lichens grew on the tree trunks. Bog vegetation included spikerushes (Eleocharis sp.), sedges (Carex sp.), both species of iris [Blue Flag (Iris versicolor) and Hooker's Iris (I. Hookeri)] and Canadian Bottlebrush (Sanguisorba Canadensis). A one inch tan butterfly with a dark pattern across the front of all wings hovered in the trails and sat with wings flat. This was the Hemlock Looper (Lambdina fiscellaria). A 1.5-inch caterpillar of the Hemlock looper hung by a thread, tan with a black diamond pattern. Mushrooms included a thin red one; a large flat topped one, a white vase-shape Clavellia and an orange 3" dome with white/yellow spots Fly Agarica (Aminita muscaria). Snail or slug tracks were on rocks across the trail.

I drove to Silver Mine Road. The road was the old road to the munitions area with all the bunkers. I did not find the silver mine this time but drove past the site of a nickel smelter. I wonder if anyone looked for uranium in the mine area. The mine produced more lead and nickel than silver. Lead/silver is often associated with uranium, and uranium is often associated with radon, which may be present in basements and houses.

At the top of the road was a blueberry barren with blueberries, what we used to call Reindeer Moss now called Caribou lichen (Cladina stellaris), heather (Calluna vulgaris), and Black Crowberry (Empetrum nigrum).

I left the old base and drove to Fox Harbor. The road was paved but it still had really steep hills. I stopped and talked to some fishermen who had just got in and were tending their nets. They gave me half an Iceland

Cockle (<u>Clinocardium cillatrum</u>) and starfish and found some large Deep Sea Scallop shells (<u>Placopecten magellanicus</u>).

The road used to stop at Fox Harbor but now continued to Ship Harbor and on to the site of the signing of the North Atlantic Charter by Roosevelt and Churchill in 1942. The Treaty park site was about 5km on east of Ship Harbor. The beach was a steep gravel/cobble slope about twenty feet high. There were broken mussel shells and some periwinkles and green urchins (<u>Stronglycentrotus droebachiensis</u>) with a bite out of the side. This indicated feeding by seals.

I returned to the hotel and went out to find cod tongues for super.

The temperatures have been unusually high in the upper 20s (80s F). Everyone was waiting for cooler weather. Lows have been in the teens. Yesterday several schools closed when the temperatures hit 30°C (86°F) and kids were complaining and getting sick. Gander had a record high of 27°C (80°F).

Day 7, 17 Sep 2003. The morning was foggy at 11°C. I headed roughly south along Hwy 100 to Cape St. Mary's. I stopped along the beach to look for shells and plants. Small horsetails (<u>Equisetum arvense</u>) and a creeping plant, Spearwort (<u>Ranuncuus flammula</u>), grew at the water's edge.

The roadside was lined with Japanese Knotweed (<u>Polygonum cuspidatum</u>) and a white wooden fence for cattle and sheep. Fences were required in the mid 1980's to keep livestock off the roads. Forty years ago there were a few sheep and cows but plenty of horses. The horses seem to have vanished.

A few older houses were painted in bright colors. Most of the new ones look like beached icebergs covered in white vinyl siding with colored trim. The siding contains insulation and has an advertised advantage of needing no painting for 20 years. The color is counterproductive since it reflects heat and negates solar heating. The vinyl also changes color and cracks over time. The change from colored houses has changed the basic looks of the communities and the ambiance of the island.

The same goes for the boats. One of the winter occupations for a fisherman was building a new boat of wood and installing the 50-year-old Atlantic 2-cycle engine. Forty years ago I suggested to a village priest that the wooden boats could be covered with fiberglass but he thought this would destroy the culture and the poor fisherman would just stay drunk.

So now there are fiberglass boats many of which are made off island and new outboards that don't last for fifty years. And today's fishermen drink less than their fathers.

I stopped in Ship Cove looking for Norm Tobin but could find no one. He was strong into environmental work.

I stopped at St Brides for a snack and information. The old folks from Angels Cove were long gone. Their kids were around but I had never met them.

A pair of White-throated Sparrows was in a native rose bush.

Outside of St Brides began blueberry barrens. The road to the Cape St Mary's Ecological Reserve ran 13 km through the barrens. Along the roadside were Pearly Everlasting, goldenrod and yarrow and bloomed out Fireweed (<u>Epilobium</u> <u>angustifolium</u>). The barrens were covered with the caribou lichen, true mosses, cotton grass, blueberries flags and several species of little wildflowers. Ancient ridges or glacial berms supported hazel (<u>Corylus</u> <u>cornuta</u>), birch (<u>Betula</u> <u>papyifera</u>), and small conifers.

The Reserve visitor center was outstanding. The dioramas and other displays were well done. The personnel were knowledgeable and helpful.

It was about noon, and the fog was not lifting so I went to see the birds anyway. A half-mile walk led to Bird Rock with hundreds of Gannets and their young. You could hear the gabbling Gannets and smell the chicken house odor before you arrived. Remarkable. You can sit just a few feet away and watch them closely. I found a Lady Tresses (<u>Habenaria</u> <u>lacera</u>) orchid on the way back to the Center.

On the way back to the highway a Merlin (<u>Falco</u> <u>columbarius</u>) with its white rump was coasting over the barrens looking for lunch.

Out by Cape St Mary's

Out on the barren
Soaring over
Blueberries and Blue Flags
Partridgeberries and crowberries
Caribou lichens and mosses

A Merlin with a white rump
Stops and hovers
Folds its wings
And drops on lunch.

*   *   *

I left about 1400 heading up Rte 92 to North Harbor and Colinet. It was roughly 75 km down a wooded ridge overlooking miles of barrens. While the dominant roadside weed group along Rte 100 was hazel, goldenrod and purple aster the dominant species along Rte 92 was Pearly Everlasting (<u>Anaphalis margaritacea</u>). A squirrel dashed across the road and a Robin burst out of the alders.

I passed through Colinet and stopped at Salmonier. I found that Mike Nolan died last year and his wife several years before. Mike was largely responsible for me getting into wildlife and ecology. We hunted Ptarmigan (<u>Lagopus</u> <u>lagopus</u>), fished and watched after his caribou and fish weirs. I traded cigarettes to his wife for fresh bread.

Highways 90 and 10 took me to St. Mary's, across the levees to Trepassey, past the archeological site near Ferryland, and up the coast to Witless Bay and Bay Bulls. Highway Rte 3 took me around Petty Harbor and Cape Spear into Mount Pearl and St John's.

Once in downtown St John's it took several trips around the block to find the B&B on Duckworth Street. I checked in and went out for supper. Fish and chips.

A cruise ship was in and there were more people on the streets than I had seen in St John's the 18 months I was here. There were a few new buildings but many of the old structures were still standing. The businesses have changed.

Day 8, 18 Sep 2003. During breakfast I found some fellow guests were playing in a Canada-wide golf tournament or running a marathon. I was not into golf and not remembered any golf courses but the course at St John's was over 100 years old. Newfoundland was in the international sports circuit.

After breakfast I went walking down Water Street to find the Downhomer magazine office. I stopped in several shops along the way

19

looking at local art and souvenirs. One of the biggest changes in the past ten years was the absence of fish flakes for drying cod from the village scenes, along with the presence of fiberglass boats with outboards, and the presence of white houses. Not old Newfoundland.

One of the editors of the Downhomer indicated they might be publishing in the next 18 months but for now they were a magazine only. Another editor said he would be happy to consider the information I developed on Newfoundland.

I wandered around some more and found where Marty's deli had been was located. This was a favorite hangout in 1960. It was now a furniture store. The boarding houses were long gone under the freeway and a couple hotels. Gone were the families that had lived dockside off of Water Street. No one would have gone to the areas where the cruise ships now dock. That was where the French and Portuguese long liners docked.

St. John's Houses

The houses along Gower Street
Red, yellow, green and brown
Show the historic character
Of this 500-year-old town

*   *   *

I returned to my room about 1100 to make some phone calls. The health department said Newfoundland had been named as the most overweight of the provinces with 59% of the adults and 36% of the kids overweight. Type 2 diabetes was getting to be a problem, particularly the juvenile kind, with 6% of the population being diabetic. Recent research had shown that the earlier children get off breast-feeding and on to cereal-based foods the higher the potential for Type 1 diabetes. Social changes may result in physiological responses.

I talked to Mines and Energy about the silver mine at Argentia and power generation for the island. The Argentia mine was mostly lead but this raises a question since there is a sign on the Back Country trail at Argentia that names a nickel smelter and a potential for radon. Most of the power was hydroelectric for Newfoundland and Labrador with one small oil-fired plant.

The Department of Agriculture had recently moved to Cornerbrook leaving a skeleton crew in St John's. I asked about tree farms and was told the paper companies were doing some planting. There was no Master Gardener program in Newfoundland. I asked about Christmas tree farming and bee keeping. There was a growing Christmas tree industry. I asked about the renting of Christmas trees that was done in St John's in the early 1960s but no one had heard of this recently. The Parks Department raised and rented potted Christmas trees for a couple weeks over Christmas. Bee keeping formerly consisted of replacement of the colonies every year. Two major bee diseases resulted in a prohibition on importing bees, so some effort to feed the bees over the winter had become necessary. Dairy farming had grown to 42 producers. They provided 95% of the milk used on Island valued at almost $30 million. Beef production was only about 2% of the demand. Sheep production provided about 15% of the domestic lamb and mutton market. There were 11 registered egg producers with about 350,000 laying hens. Chicken producers raised over 9 million chickens a year. Greenhouse vegetables amounted to about $9 million. Field-raised vegetable production was about 1800 acres worth about $4 million.

Fisheries and forestry people had moved to Cornerbrook and were not available.

I walked out to Churchill Square near Memorial University to visit the Barrington bookstore. No poetry is planned for the next few weeks. Most of the students visible in Churchill Square area were co-eds in groups of two to six. None of these appeared to cruise Water Street like 40 years before looking for a GI like the 40,000 girls who did marry servicemen since 1940.

There was a Laundromat a few blocks from the B&B. I got a sack with a week's clothes in by noon and they were ready by 1500. Twelve dollars.

The Hubleys owned a plumbing shop up the street. I asked about Clary Hubley whom I had known. His nephew told me that Clary had died two years before of Parkinson's and cancer.

The host at the B&B recommended supper at Chuckys. It was about three blocks mostly downhill. I had chowder and a seal flipper pie. The pie was much better than my last go around with flippers. It still had a strong taste similar to kidney pie with a few flat bones. Moose and caribou were on the menu along with cod and halibut.

Fish and Brewis and Flippers, too

I first tried the national dish of Newfoundland,
fish and brewis, at the start of the day
in the fishing village of Fox Harbor
on frigid Argentia Bay.

The eastern light was just breaking
when the smell of a kerosene lamp
and hot lard filled the cabin
and waken the rest of the camp.

The fish—Bacalao or Morue
(other names for salted cod)—
had been soaked, rinsed, sliced
and was frying in hot lard.

Brewis was sea biscuits or hard tack
out of the tin dry and hard.
It was soaked and sliced,
and boiled or fried in the hot fish flavored lard.

This was the solstice morning.
Breakfast special was flippers of seal
that had soaked in milk over night
to make it a palatable meal.

The flippers were smothered in onions
and placed in the wood stove's oven
It baked for an hour and began to smell
like something from a witches coven.

Fish and brewis is some good
but flippers with flat bones like those in your hand?
Imagine the taste beef liver boiled in fish oil.
It didn't quite fit into my plan.

Out of the warm, smoky cabin

> the crisp morning air feels so nice
> on a beach of cobbles the size of soft balls
> and crystal clear water cold as ice.

*   *   *

Day 9, 19 Sep 2003. I checked out, moved my stuff out to the car and walked two blocks to a bank. There I bought enough Technicolor Canadian dollars for the weekend. I turned in the room key and my temporary parking permit and headed out Duckworth Street to Signal Hill.

Signal Hill was a fortification overlooking the entrance to St. John's harbor. The canons that protected the harbor had been restored. The most prominent structure, Cabot Tower, was built in 1897 for the Diamond Jubilee of Queen Victoria and the 400th anniversary of discovery. The tower was used by Marconi as a site for receiving the first trans-Atlantic wireless signal on 12 Dec 1901.

When I was there in 1960 the archeology had just begun and the area where the cannons are located was a favorite parking spot. A couple of local lasses and a bottle of Screech and we were set for the evening. There was a tale of the wandering ghost of a fisherman with an axe. He was said to have caught his daughter and some guy up on Signal Hill and had murdered then in a fit of rage. This made the spot even more of an adventure to see the ghost. We saw someone crossing over the hill one night and made sure the doors were locked. We left in a cloud of dust as soon as the figure disappeared.

Pepperell Air Base was closed in 1960 but was still clearly visible from Signal Hill with the housing area shaped like a cowboy hat. The old Officers Club and bowling alley were still in operation.

About noon I left for north or Atlantic side to Pouch Cove then down the east side of Conception Bay through Portugal Cove, Paradise, and Topsail Beach to Holyrood. Belle Island with its iron mines sat off the coast in the middle of the Bay.

Holyrood was much larger than I remembered. The train memorials were new but back then the train was in operation. The freezer plan was still in operation but the chief products were no longer squid and blueberries. Other fish products and red berries were now the major products.

I took Hwy 60 to Brigus to Hwy 70 to Bay Roberts. Brigus had always been one of my favorite towns. I was getting sleepy and cut over on Hwy 73 to New Harbor and the B&B at Dildo.

The B&B recommended a restaurant for supper. My first Fish and Brewis in 40 years. Desert was a berry cobbler with fresh whipped cream. Very good.

The low road along the bay at Dildo ran along the shore for several kilometers. The beach is a typical cobble beach. Abandoned and old fish stages inhabit the shore. Whales could be seen in the bay but not while I was there.

B&Bs are different. Some people seem to enjoy running one while others are in it for the money. Some are decorated nicely, some cutesy, others are strictly utilitarian.

Day 10, 20 Sep 2003. I got up about 0700 and went for a walk along the beach. The whelks and a few broken mussel shells were on the beach and live Littorina were living on exposed rocks. There were remains of abandoned fish stages and rusted equipment since fishing had been cut back. Many years ago when the salt cod market crashed schooners were abandoned on the beach.

I left Dildo about 0930 to meet the Trans Canada Highway. Once past Blakestown the goldenrod and bottlebrush returned to the roadside. Mist alternated with light rain.

A bunch of classic vehicles passed. A 2000K-road rally was underway ending in St John's.

I came to Clarenville about noon and got on Hwy 230 for Bonavista. I stopped at a farmers market near Lethbridge. Mr. Robertson was a Yank with a local wife. His parents lived in Palestine, Texas. He farmed about 70 acres and produced cold-adapted varieties of beets, turnips, carrots, potatoes, cabbage, broccoli, zucchini, pumpkin, raspberries and blueberries and bicolor corn.

There were some birch trees cut for firewood. A lot of little Eyebright (Euphrasia sp.) was present in the turf.

I arrived at Bonavista about 1400 and found the B&B. After check-in I went out to the lighthouse on Cape Bonavista. The lighthouse was being repaired after a fire destroyed a recent repair job. A moss, Awned Hair-cap

(Polytrichum piliferum) and Common or Prostrate Juniper (Juniperus communis) were growing in the rocks along with several tiny wildflowers.

I stopped to see the statue of Cabot and went looking for sea caves called the Dungeon the returned back to town. Next stop was to see the Mathew, a locally built replica of Cabot's caravel. It was after 1700 so stopped for supper. Fresh salmon.

Day 11, 21 Sep 2003. The morning was overcast and still for a change at 9°C. I walked the beach and found a few shells and a Sea-Rocket (Cakile edentula) partially covered with Wrack. For some reason it was a pink color. I also found pieces of Irish Moss (Chondrus crispus).

I took Hwy 235 to Hwy 230 at Southern Bay and on down to Clarenville. The TCH took me back south to Hwy 210 to Marystown.

A ground squirrel darted out into the road and stopped in front of the car. Squirrel burger. Sure hate that but it's the fate of the dumb or slow.

I stopped at Leathbridge for gas. It was 90 cents/liter and cost $41.00.

When I took this road in 1960 it was one lane gravel and foggy with a visibility of half mile or less. Today was clear blue and sharp. Temperature was about 18° (61°F).

About 20 miles along the vegetation changed from woods to barrens. The barrens still tickle me. Trudge up hill and there is a pond. I know this is a result of glacial sculpting but it still feels strange. There were several feet of peat but little soil. There were hammocks or ridges where enough soil exists to support trees. The peat supported blueberries, caribou lichen and other similar bog plants. The saturated mulch holds water. Bog iron nodules were common.

The water was cold and clear and supports a limited variety of plants and animals like diatoms. Years ago two of us went camping in the middle of the Avalon. We got hot after walking a couple hours with packs and decided to take a swim and cool down. We stripped down and climbed in. The water was cold and felt good for a few minutes. Getting out of the pond was difficult with the slimy diatoms on the rocks. We were covered with a reddish muck.

At least there were no mosquitoes or deer flies this trip.

Mosquitoes in My Motel Room

When I opened the door and turned on the light
mosquitoes were lurking just waiting to bite.

I swatted and squashed for a minute or two
and they disappeared right into the blue.

I turned on the sink and flushed out a couple
and one from the overflow compounded my trouble.

When I turned on the tub three more were washed out
and two more flew out of the drain with a pout.

They hid in the drapes and under the chairs
and hummed about blood that soon would be theirs.

Stop! I can't take any more.
I threw on some clothes and ran out the door

to find a bug bomb
to kill these blood sucking ladies and even their mom.

I sprayed half a can. There. That should be enough
that is, if these swamp ladies were not super tough.

I backed out the door to wait 'til they died
but out in the courtyard was one I could ride

so I ran for the car and left the same night
straight back to West Texas where tall tales don't bite.

*   *   *

Much of the rock is Precambrian basalt with quartz and iron inclusions.

An intrusion into the landscape was local electrical distribution lines and high voltage towers. They were seldom out of sight for the whole ride.

Pickups and cars were parked along the roads as people were picking berries, cutting wood and hunting moose. I met several groups of motorcycles also. This was a big change since the 60s when many people had no vehicle, and many had never been outside the village.

A stretch about a mile long supported a stand of birch trees. Birch appears to be one of the primary fire wood species.

Even along this relatively deserted road people appear to be power walking for exercise, mostly women. Some were walking the dog. Most of the walking men appeared to be going somewhere specific.

I stopped to look at a pond. A small shrub called Meadowsweet (Spirea latifolia) was in bloom. The Fragrant Water Lily (Nymphacea ordorata) plants were not in bloom.

Fellow guests at the Bonavista B&B from Toronto remarked how primitive Newfoundland was with wood frame buildings and relative simple roads. They also remarked on the lack of birds and animals. I saw it from a different perspective. They did not notice the white color of the buildings, or the presence of roads and power poles. Or the number of vehicles. Or running water and flush toilets. Or telephones and TVs. Or that the picturesque dock out into the bay did not have an outhouse on the end. Or the near complete lack of the old fashion dories. Or looked behind the walls of an old house to find lath from lobster pots and layers of fifty-year-old newspapers to keep out the wind.

A small river had a solar powered flow monitoring station with a microwave link.

I arrived at Marystown and found the hotel about 1400. Marystown had a major shipyard and fish processing plant.

After checking in I drove to Grand Banks, Fortune, and Burin. The trip took about three hours. Grand Banks had a long history and an active waterfront. It was the site of the Fisherman's Museum.

On the way to Fortune a large trawler passed on a flat sea. Outstanding. The trip around the end of the world was uneventful. I could see the French islands of St. Pierre and Miquelon in the distance and their local radio station played French songs. About 15 km of road was under construction and rough and dusty.

People of the Village of Lawn were important actors in a US Navy disaster during WWII. Three US ships ran aground in a storm with few survivors. The people of Lawn rescued and cared for many of the ships crewmembers. One of the survivors was one of the first African Americans to be seen in the area.

Just past St Lawrence was a dam and hydroelectric generator. Further on was a lake called Salt Pond surrounded by cabins and campers. I bypassed Fortune but it looked like an interesting town for future visits.

Day 12, 22 Sept 2003. The morning was 13°C and foggy with visibility of about a half mile. I drove along listening to CBC radio. A new UN study on sustainable forestry sounded interesting. Seems like corruption and politics were the major problems. Allowing scientific guidance to be superceded by political decisions is dumb but might interfere with getting reelected.

By 1000 I was back on the TCH headed for Terra Nova National Park. Not much traffic and a 100-kph speed limit. I stopped at several visitor information sites and found them closed. One that was open this morning explained that those marked with large black question marks were open seven days and the little question marks were open weekdays only. So? This was Monday and they were not open.

The TCH through the park was like the rest of the highway but there were subtle differences in the woods and hills. The Terra Nova interpretative center was manned by two helpful ladies but without scientific guidance. I took the self-guided tour and sat through an excellent movie then bought some books on birds and plants and headed for Gander. According to the Park maps there were several interesting trails but the time was not available. The hills and the rest of Newfoundland were part of the Appalachian Mountain system. The rounded hills were the result of repeated glaciations.

CBC was discussing making voting compulsory either by fines or by tax credits. This seemed to work in several countries. They were also discussing giving volunteers like firemen and emergency medics an income tax credit for a minimum of 200 hours a year. This might encourage volunteerism.

I stopped at the Joey Smallwood overlook over the Gambo Valley. This was an important lumber and fishing region and, beginning about 1900, a tourist destination.

I was near Gander by 1330 and stopped at the forestry interpretive center, which turned out to be unmanned. Common trees are Black

Spruce (<u>Picea mariana</u>), White Spruce (<u>Picea glauca</u>), Larch (<u>Larix laricina</u>), Balsam Fir (<u>Abies balsamea</u>), white pine (<u>Pinus strobus</u>), White Birch (<u>Betula pendula</u>), and Aspen (<u>Populus tremuloides</u>).

I went into Gander and out to the airport to talk about bird strikes. The airport had been a Canadian Air Force base and had been the site of many historic flights. It had been important during WWII. I had spent the night on the base in 1960 on my way to Argentia.

Common plants along the 40 km Hwy 330 towards Gander Bay were Everlasting, birch, alder, rumex, goldenrod, and bloomed out Fireweed. Several roadside ditches contained cattails.

A road sign warned of moose. Canada in general has a shortage of road signs and street signs. It's probably a money problem. Highway markers are miles apart. Many villages are not marked but then they have few houses. Most of the cross roads are marked but the main roads or streets are not. The roads are pretty good shape considering the snow and temperature changes.

I went out Hwy 331 to 340 and turned towards Boyd's Cove to the Beothuk archeological center. An interesting diorama and displays and a good video preceded a 1.5km walk through the wood to the site. Representative plants were marked and the trail was well maintained. The primary site contained 14 depressions representing pits for lodges or other structures. Four had been excavated and over 12,000 artifacts had been recorded. No further excavation was projected. The area had been mapped in detail.

A bridge across the stream near the site crossed a deep pothole. This depression looked possibly artificial and had probably been used to hold water and maybe to trap spawning runs of fish. A couple of high peaks in the area would have made good outlooks. Archaic Indian and Inuit sites had been found as well as the Beothuk site proving that great minds think alike.

I would recommend looking in the pothole and doing some prescribed burns to remove liter and downed timber and to allow better access to the surface. Probably won't happen. I was familiar with the complications dealing with state and national historic preservation organizations and native groups.

There was a Robin hopped across the trail and a Black-capped Chickadee flew into the shrubs along the trail.

Back to Hwy 340. It would have been interesting to go right and take the ferry to the Change Islands and Fogo but that is for another trip.

I was at the Brittany Inn in Lewisporte by 1830. I had a shrimp dinner in the dining room.

Lewisporte was a former important link to Labrador and to St. Anthony. It was still a shipping center and big into private boating but not like when it connected the railroad to the Labrador and the eastern shore. The area is also a center for fishing and hunting.

Day 13, 23 Sep 2003. Today is the first day of fall. Lewisporte was overcast in with no wind and 11°C. I left about 0900 for a short run to the TCH. I went on up to Grand Banks then north to Hwy 350 to Roberts Arm. The area around Grand Banks had been cut and looked like some had been reforested since some of the trees were nice enough to grow in straight lines. Roadside trees were unorganized.

Road signs again. One sign will say Grand Banks with an arrow. A bit down the road will be a second sign will say Grand Banks with the mileage. Why not just one sign?

There were weighing stations for trucks. I assume this was to prevent overloaded trucks from destroying the roads. Or could it be for tax purposes.

Along the road were some large leafed succulent plant, Coltsfoot (Tussilago farfara), a small Canada Thistle (Cirsium arvense), and Curled Dock (Rumex crispus).

I finally arrived at Roberts Arm and drove down to the dock area. Three coastal trawlers were ready to go. The harbor bottom around the dock was littered with scallop and mussel shells. I talked a minute to an old man who answered in monosyllables. Sounds like home.

I went back to the high road and east to the end of the road. Next village was Pilley's Island with a causeway. Numerous floats of a large Blue Mussel farm occupied much of the surface. Then on to Triton/Jim's Cove/Card's Harbor and Brighton on Notre Dame Bay. Many new homes indicated a growing economy.

I stopped at Fudges Restaurant in Triton for lunch. Three big fresh stuffed squid. Delicious.

Next stop was at the general store. It had groceries like Fritos, canned goods and one bunch of bananas, plastic chairs and some clothing.

Another similar store in Roberts Arm had about the same items plus hardware, paint and floor coverings.

I checked into the only local motel. The room was at ambient and the baseboard electric heaters took several hours to bring the temperature to my livable 25°C. This was an efficiency room with stove, and dishes.

Day 14, 24 Sep 2003. Overcast again. I was off at 0830. Roberts Arm had three stores, a motel, a snack bar, a gas station and garage.

I was on the TCH a little after 0900. It was about 150 km to Deer Lake and another 30 km to Wiltondale. Should be there right after lunch.

I stopped at the tourist information office and asked about the Baie Verte (Green Bay). The attendant said she had never been there but that there was an Inuit pipe stone quarry at Fluer de Lys and an open-pit asbestos mine. These sounded interesting so I went up Hwy 410.

A black weasel came out of the bushes, stopped, looked and turned back.

CBC announced: the temperature was 13; there was a large iceberg off Twillingate and St Anthony; the International Forestry Management conference was being held in Montreal and the Newfoundland/Inuit forest management plan for Labrador had been announced.

This route was called the Dorset Trail for the Dorset Eskimos. I stopped at the visitor center at Baie Verte and picked up some minerals from the their sample pile. Small blue Bluets (<u>Hedyotis (Houstonia) caerulea</u>) were in bloom around the building. The gift shop had a T-shirt for Screech but not in my size. Screech was a Jamaican rum long favored as the national bootleggers choice.

I stopped at the asbestos overlook. Big hole. Lots of loose asbestos ore.

The Dorset site and museum were well executed. Nice little museum. The site had been excavated and artifacts of archaic settlers 8000 years back were found along with Paleo-Inuit artifacts over 2000 years old. The Inuit had carved around the proposed soapstone vessel, then under cut the object and broke it off. It was then hollowed out to make a bowl of sorts.

A Blue Jay was screeching as it flew between the trees. Several other birds flew in the distance or flitted across the road. One was finch size. The others were possibly Robins.

Harebell (<u>Campanula rotundifolia</u>) and Creeping Buttercup (<u>Ranunculus repens</u>) grew at the site with Goldenrod and Fall Dandelion.

One of the local fishermen mentioned that a group of American Elderhostellers had been in town. He also said humpback whales came into the harbor around the beginning of October and stayed until Christmas; pods of Killer Whales came into the bay in the winter for a few days and moved on; his brother had worked in Houston for over twenty years coming home a couple times a year.

I drove back to the TCH and headed west. Both Birchy and Sandy Lakes were down about 6-8 feet. This was partly due to a drought that had many ponds down a foot or so but mostly from drawdown for hydroelectric generation.

The turn off from TCH to Hwy 430/Viking Trail at Deer Lake was under construction and directions were not clear. I was on the Viking Trail by 1430 and checked in my motel at Wiltondale by 1500.

It was still early so I took the Gros Morne park road towards Trout River. A slow rain was falling. The park road and scenery was much like the rest of the roads so far. The park actually had a lot of houses, several small towns, churches, cemeteries, etc. I stopped at the visitor center for park maps and information then drove on to Trout River. The table or flat top mountains were to the left and a green valley to the right and the rain was all over. There was supposed to be some farming in the valley.

The large-leafed plant called Coltsfoot grew along the road. It had yellow flower stalks in the spring that moose eat. Later in the year the moose eat the large leaves.

It was raining harder at Trout River. I drove around town and stopped for a supper of Wolf Fish. I took a short walked along the beach in the drizzle and found nothing. Not even seaweed.

On the return drive three cow moose were in the road in the rain. With cars approaching from both directions they ambled off the road.

The room had a TV but no signal. I decided one night there was enough. In the morning I would drive through Gros Morne National Park. I might take the fiord boat ride up Western Brook Pond if it cleared up and then go on north for the night.

Day 15, 25 Sep 2003. About 0400 the sky was clear and the stars bright. Polaris was nearly overhead. It was foggy by sun up.

I left about 0800 and drove to Rocky Harbor. This village had a lighthouse and a dock and lots of white houses, a chain motel and a couple of restaurants. A combination gift shop and liquor store had some miniature bottles of Screech but no Screech T-shirt. They wanted $39 for a liter of Screech.

I booked a ride on the boat on Western Brook Pond. It left at 1300 but there was a 4 km walk to it. It was only 0930 so no hurry.

A short walk along the beach yielded nothing new but there were a number of green and yellow land snails (<u>Capaea</u> <u>hortensis</u>) feeding on Coltsfoot.

One of the hills had a sign for trucks to test their brakes. A road sign warned trucks to use a low gear. Newfoundland always had steep hills but most were not marked. Regular hills were low gear hills. It used to be a joke that on the ones marked steep you drove down in reverse.

I stopped at a lighthouse built in 1897. Before this each family on the cove donated a pint of oil a week to keep one lamp lit.

Tuckamore. These are mostly Black Spruce trees whose new growth gets frozen back resulting in stunted trees. They grow thick and many of the lower limbs are gone. Vegetation under the tuckamore included mosses, Snowberry, Buttercup and other shade tolerant plants. Groves of these trees occurred along the coast and across the open bogs exposed to the north wind.

Another stop was at an old fishing camp on Broom Point. Inuits had used it for several hundred years followed by the Basque and others. One family used it for almost a hundred years until 1975 when the point became part of the park. The camp had a barn and two houses and a fish stage. There were fish flakes and traps for crabs and lobsters for display. A guided tour was available but no one was home.

I drove back to the parking area for the boat ride and started the hike about 1100. The trail went over three treed limestone ridges and around a couple ponds and extensive bogs. Wetlands included carnivorous plants like sundew and bladderwort.

I took the extra kilometer loop through the woods. There were moose tracks and a pile of moose droppings that were summer brown instead of winter straw color. There were also two piles of red-brown mush mixed with berries. Moose puke?

Along the trail were a lot of Coltsfoot and berries and several stands of Cow Parsnip (<u>Heracleum</u> <u>maximum</u>). Gnarled birch trees were a good 18" in diameter. Creeping Anemone, Joe-Pye Weed, Everlasting and Goldenrod grew where it was dry. Daucus and the Purple Aster were invasives. Bogs had Sweetgale (<u>Myrica</u> <u>gale</u>), Labrador Tea (<u>Ledum</u> <u>groenlandicum</u>), Sheep Laurel (<u>Kalmia</u> <u>angustifoliua</u>), Bottlebrush, Blue Flags, Cotton Grass (<u>Eriophorum</u> sp,) and Bluejoint Grass/Marsh Reed Grass (<u>Calamagrostis</u> <u>Canadensis</u>). There was some bloomed out Cow Parsnip. There was a big bracket fungus, Birch Maze-gill (<u>Lenzites</u> <u>betulina</u>), on a down birch tree. Canadian Thistle was stunted and had lots of sharp points. Some Witches Broom grew in the Spruce.

I finally heard the boat then saw the building. They had moved one boat in on a sled. A second larger boat was flown in in pieces. The pond is a relic fiord about 16 miles long with walls up to 2200 ft and is 575 ft deep. Conductivity was very low and pH 7.

The little tan butterfly, the Hemlock Looper, appeared in the Spruce. At the landing an aggressive Gray Jay dive-bombed food from people's hands.

The trip was from 1300 to 1530. Interesting but pretty chilly. We went out across the lake and up the fiord looking at coves and waterfalls and rockslides to the upper end. At the far end we picked up a hiker who had completed the cross-country hike from Gros Morne.

I drove up to Port au Choix for the night. I found a room at a Jennies B&B next to a cemetery. Quiet neighbors.

So far I have had an iron bed, a sleigh bed, a brass bed, and several inconsequential beds.

Day 16, 26 Sep 2003. The night was clear with Mars shining brightly. No northern lights. A cloudbank on the horizon turned pink as sunrise approached.

The claim to fame for Port au Choix was really old gravesites. The host said her father had found several skeletons when he built the house and more were found when the beauty shop was built next door. Port au Choix was named because of the choice of three anchorages but the area was an island until the land rebound after the last glacial period. Apparently the natives liked to bury their dead in islands or hilltops. Hundreds of burial sites had been identified from Maritime Archaic about 5000 years ago, the Groswater Paleo-Eskimos 2800-1900 years BC, 3000 years back the Dorset Inuit, then paleo-Indians and Europeans about 1000 AD.

There was an interpretive center for the gravesites. The lighthouse was a working lighthouse. Shale shingle on the beach contained fossil ammonites and trilobites.

A Harebell and a Chinese Mustard (<u>Brassica juncea</u>), each about 3 inches tall, were struggling out of the shale. It was cold and windy and they are in bloom.

I bought some Bakeapple preserves at the visitor center. First I had seen. I was told the harvest had been scant and most of the jelly and preserves had been sold out.

Down around the lighthouse I found several partial fossils. They called this the French Shore since the area had been in dispute several times.

Flowers included Yarrow, a Prostrate Juniper, clover, grasses, etc. There were some glacial leftovers—granite cobbles abraded almost round as and about the size of basketballs. Seaweed including Wrack and Bladder Wrack was washed up on shore. There was some plastic pieces including rope and netting. Wind was from the south at 18k.

Back in town I stopped at a bank to buy more local colored currency. Rate was 1.32 down from 1.44.

Along the highway the trees grew to full size. Everlasting, Cow Parsnip, and Fall Dandelion lined the road.

I stopped to look at some sleds for hauling logs probably drawn by Skidoo. Forty years before horses would have pulled the sleds.

There were gardens along the edge of the road surrounded by a fence and hung with all sorts of stuff that was supposed to chase the birds. These gardens were in barrens with muck soil and the bog water supply. They raised potatoes, onions, zucchini, carrots, beets, turnips, cabbage and such.

I turned on to Hwy 432 across the peninsula to Main Brook and on to the St Anthony airport. The Birches were bright yellow near the center of the peninsula where it was higher and the temperature fluctuated more than along the coast.

Back on Hwy 430 I drove into St. Anthony. No information center. Museum and craft center closed. Hospital and Salvation Army. It was Friday afternoon and nobody home.

I backtracked to Hwy 437 and charged on to L'anse aux Meadows. Barrens were really rocky and barren. Firewood was piled along the road. I stopped at a jelly stand where a young man had started selling his mothers jelly several years before. He was now a fisherman gone for a month at a time to Greenland fishing for turbot.

I checked in at Marilyn's B&B. She recommended I go to Norsted first since it was the last day of their season.

Norsted was a reproduction of a Norse trading village. Replicas of different kinds of buildings had been built in the Norse style of timber covered with sod. This was an interpretive center with actors dressed in Norse dress, playing character roles, and demonstrating crafts. The boathouse held a Viking ship that had been built for some celebration. The ship had been given to Canada who had no immediate use for it. It was given to the Norsted center for safekeeping. A couple of guides were very informative.

The beach was sprinkled with mussel shells and broken whelks, periwinkles and green sea urchin shells. Gulls pick the shells up and drop them on the rocks.

I had scallops for supper with iceberg ice in the water. The ice was clear but full of gas. Little bubbles of 10,000-year-old air came out as the ice melted. I saw iceberg ice for sale at $5/kilo.

Around the restaurant were Spikewort, Everlasting, Yarrow, a couple of grasses, Rumex, and Bottlebrush. In one of the gardens grew a large white daisy and a Gaillardia still in bloom.

Back at the B&B we watched TV and talked of many things. Land prices and new housing cost was ridiculous. Lots ran $10K to $50K or more. Houses like 3000 sq ft plus a basement were $150-300 thousand. Sale value depended on location. Locally a 3000 sq ft house could be had for $30K. The difference was in philosophy. The U.S. looked at a house as an investment to be eventually sold while Newfoundlanders looked at a house as possession with no intent of ever getting rid of it.

We also discussed birthdays. Almost every Newfoundlander I had known had been born in the July or August. This backdates to October/November when the fishing season ended and before the first snow began when they could begin cutting and hauling timber. This did not apply as strictly as in the past and families with ten or more children that lived were no longer common.

Day 17, 27 Sep 2003. I looked out the window about 0200. It was clear and the stars were out. It was overcast by dawn.

I checked out after breakfast and went to the archeological site of the first known European settlement on North America. The displays were very good. Artifacts from the site included nails and slag from smelting bog iron and a bronze pin that pretty much proved it was Viking. A relief map of the site gave a different perspective to the relationships of the land 1000 years ago compared to today's view out the windows. The land had rebounded over the past thousand years once the weight of ice age glaciers had been removed. There were many interpretive displays and a diorama representing a scene in front of the long house. The personnel were very helpful. There was a good overview of the site from the center's windows.

At the actual excavation site there were 14 sites and four had been excavated. Replicas of several buildings had been built and interpretive tours were conducted. I went out to the site for a look just as it started raining. No tour was available.

I left and drove along Hwy 430 in the rain. Much of the trip across the top of the peninsula was through barrens that were literally just rock. No tuckamore. No Blueberries. Lots of Bakeapples. Almost 50km with no structures. A warning sign had a Caribou instead of the Moose. Most of the signs I had seen had a Moose or a Moose nose-to-nose with a smashed car.

I stopped for a look at St. Barbe where the Labrador ferry docked. It had one motel and ticket office, a gas station and a few houses. The fog cut visibility to a half mile or less.

About 200km along was The Arches Provincial Park. This was a weather carved limestone ridge 450M years old and the arches were the remains of sea caves.

I stopped at a B&B at Shallow Bay/Cowhead for the night. Nice room with an ocean view.

The beach was not accessible. I walked down the road past the hotel to a church that had a wildflower garden with some of the local flora identified. Large black bees were working on the flowers. A flock of English Sparrows was congregating in a shrub. On the way back I stopped at the motel dining room for scallops.

The B&B was owned by the motel on down the street. The motel had acquired the land and decided to rent it out as a B&B instead of expanding the motel complex.

I noticed when I went to change the temperature in the room that the highest temperature was 24°C (65°F). That's one way to conserve electricity.

Day 18, 28 Sep 2003. I woke at 0200 and 0430 to look at the stars. The sky was clear and black with sparkling stars. The Big Dipper was up north pointing south to Polaris almost overhead. Scorpio was to the south. Mars was reflected off a mirror-flat tidal pool. The sun came up clear, but there were mares-tails indicating a weather change coming. The radio said Hurricane Juan was headed for Halifax.

I was driving out of town when I saw a house painted green that turned out to be a museum that was not open.

Back on Hwy 430 a couple of Robins and a Striped Chipmunk with it tail held high crossed the road.

It looks like they used a hydroaxe to clear the roadside shrubbery. They were rotomilling and resurfacing several miles of the road through the park.

I noticed at least some local construction used planking over the studs instead of particleboard or plywood. Guess you use what you have available.

Next stop was almost to TCH at the Insectorium. This was one of only two in all of Canada. It was founded and run by a couple forestry people in a renovated dairy barn. They had acquired a good collection of mounted specimens and constructed some wonderful interpretive displays. They close for the winter and take the show on the road to schools and malls. They identified my two butterflies. The yellow butterfly from the windshield was an Alfalfa Sulphur. The tan one was the Hemlock looper, a forest pest

They also had a nature walk. Swamp Thistle (<u>Cirsium</u> <u>muticum</u>). Orange Hawkweed (<u>Heiracium</u> <u>aurantiacum</u>). Smaller Forget-me-not (<u>Myosotis</u> <u>laxa</u>). Eyebright. Woundwort (<u>Stachys</u> <u>palustris</u>). Strawberries in bloom. Blue Joint Grass.

I drove on past Deer Lake and Cornerbrook and found my B&B along the Humber Arm. We discussed Newfoundland, wildlife, hunting, ATVs and antiques. We sat outside in the evening cool and watched the clouds and talked more while a Blue Jay kibitzed

I mentioned the lack of antiques and antique stores in Newfoundland. Apparently the antiques left by the truckload when the roads came in the late 60s then by the boatload as the source was recognized. I remember shopping for antiques in London in the late 60s and found the affordable antiques were reproductions or were imported from Canada. Dealers had come and bought out whole village collections for next to nothing. Furniture. Fishing gear. Whatever.

Supper was a Jigs dinner with the family. Boiled beef and chicken with potatoes, carrots, cabbage and mashed turnips.

Day 19, 29 Sep 2003. The morning was cool, moist and windy. I left and turned left intending to go to Lark Harbor at the end of the world. The road was peppered with houses making the entire road one big subdivision. At Frenchman's Cove I turned around, gassed up and headed for Burgeo. There were some pretty large homes with spectacular views of the Humber Arm.

Popping over one hill there was a break in the clouds and Corner Brook was lit by the sun. Neat view. Corner Brook has a long history as a shipping center for lumber and paper but I could not see it as a tourist destination.

The local forest was speckled with bright red Maple trees and yellow Aspen and Birch. Further south the Maples disappeared.

Hundreds of gulls were grounded on the beaches at low tide. The wind was blowing 50-70 knots with a temperature of 15°C. Guess the weather was unsuitable for flying or there were no fishing boats to harass.

I turned off the TCH to go to the Stephenville airport. The turnoff was about 20 km off the TCH. The airport still looks like a US Air Force Base. The BOQ, some hangars, base housing, the gym, the theatre, and the hospital had all been converted to local use. The buildings were pastel colors and some of the large spaces on the building were covered with murals. This looked like a success story.

The operations manager told me about their bird strike program. He said they had only one strike this year. Most of the past hits had been gulls. Management mowed and had burned the infield to eliminate the rodents and other pests that attracted both hawks and gulls. They did not own a propane canon and did not see the need for one. I concur. They had a moose that stepped over the fence but St John's had had several moose. He mentioned that they kept track of a big nesting area near Stephenville Crossing.

I asked the Budget car rental people if they were interested in inspecting the car since I had put about 4000km on it. They could care less since the car belonged to Halifax and the Newfoundland franchise belonged to someone else.

There was some tall yellow Evening Primrose about a meter tall. This was Sundrops (<u>Oenothera</u> <u>perennis</u>).

The wind was blowing fiercely looking like 50kph. The radio said 50-70kph with gusts to 110kph and rain. Darn.

I bypassed Stephenville Crossing. There was an old iron railroad bridge parallel to the road across the St George River.

The sign for the road to Burgeo said 148km. One car passed me, and I met about a dozen others during the trip. Fog reduced visibility to one kilometer or less and, at times, the raincells looking like tiny white tornados walking. First time I ever saw rain cells walking across the road. A flock of ducks hit a pond at the edge of the fog. There were a couple of hunting camp settlements and even one restaurant but that was all until Burgeo.

I found the B&B and looked around town. It was relatively small and several people were walking along the road in the mist. There was a choice of three eateries, a bank, a grocery store and a museum that was closed. I went down to look at the ferry dock. Functional. The ferry serviced all the villages along the west coast between Port-au-Basque to Grand Banks.

There were two fellow guests from the University of Victoria doing sociological research. I had dinner and a beer with them.

Day 20, 30 Sep 2003. The wind was still blowing and some rain falling. Rain in sheets beat on the window sporadically during the night. This storm was tied to Hurricane Juan.

I left about 0830. Visibility was about 2-4 km in rain. T'was not a fun drive but better than yesterday. Streams were full and rushing, tumbling brown and foaming. By the time I reached the TCH it had stopped blowing and raining.

The CBC was talking about a cap on credit card interest like 5% over prime that would still allow a big profit. The risk in Canada was less than in the US. They also announced Prince Edwards Island had an 83% voter turnout. Last election in San Antonio it was barely 15%.

Several birds dashed across the road about knee high a couple hundred meters ahead. Possibly Yellow-bellied Flycatchers or Robins. Red Maples had penetrated maybe 30 KM off the TCH into the interior.

Down TCH there was little flowering vegetation. Occasional Everlasting and Fireweed.

A station was playing French songs. In 1960 I believe there was a Basque station or at least some Basque programming. It was certainly not French or Spanish. We could sometimes hear it at Argentia.

The intersection to the Codroy Valley finally arrived. I stopped at the corner convenience store to look and ask directions to the B&B. Right road and just down the road a piece. Actually I followed the road signs right to the front door.

On the way I stopped at the Codroy Valley Wetland Interpretive Center that had been started by a local schoolteacher. Nicely done.

I checked in and called the Ferry in Port-au-Basque. Departure time had changed, so I changed my reservation to the midnight run on 1 Oct. I also called the airline. They got me a flight out of Newark to Memphis at 1045 and Memphis to SA at 1245 on the 5th. It arrived in San Antonio 8 hours earlier than the previous flight.

It was early so I drove through the local villages on the north side and out to the lighthouse at Cape Anguille, the most western tip of Newfoundland.

I looked around the backyard. It was about a hundred yards of backyard to the water. Maple, horse chestnut (Aesculus sp.), and apple trees. Buttercup and clover. Eyebright. Spikewort. Mouse ears. Goldenrod.

Supper was pork chops with the family. During and after supper we discussed Newfoundland. There was no longer anything unique to the Island. Art, poetry, computer software were being produced. All the world's products were available, maybe not in the local convenience store but certainly on the Internet. Cost of living appears about the same as on the rest of Canada.

In the 1950s and 1960s there were technology gaps. There were communities accessible by boat or foot trail and isolated in the winter but they could get on the radio and talk to any one in the world or call in a helicopter for emergencies.

Property values were $2-6K per acre. The problem was that there were only parcels of 5-15 acres with no small lots available.

The host said two of his sons were in Ft McMurray and one had just bought a house. He was renting half to his brother.

We discussed the white houses. Vinyl siding had several problems. It fades. If it is not properly installed moisture and dry rot could damage the frame

Day 21, 1 Oct 2003. The morning valley was a hazy pastel of greens and tans. I drove down the southern shore past farms and fields of hay and pasture with the Grand Codroy River and the northern shore in the background. Hwy 407 went through Searston, St Andrews and Tompkins before reaching the TCH. Pastel farm scenes and wetlands and a flock of ducks blended into the haze. Out on the horizon the flat blue of the Gulf of St Lawrence met the blue of the sky.

Along this stretch of TCH were wind-warning signs. Gusts had been recorded near 200kph. That would be a really bad wind. I remember 70k gusts at Argentia that could blow you off the sidewalk not to mention a wind chill of 40 below.

I just passed a bicyclist pedaling away. I'm afraid that with the hills and wind I would be pushing the bike a lot.

As I drove past Port-au-Basque I checked the access to the ferry and took the road to Margaree, Fox Roost, Isle aux Morts, Burnt Islands, Diamond Cove, and Rose Blanche-Harbour la Cou. After three weeks on the road I finally found some of the pretty houses.

The first detour was to Margaree and Fox Roost. The colored houses were there with satellite dishes tacked to the wall and telephone and electrical connections and poles. Margaree had a wharf and a fish plant. Fox Roost had cars, kids and a few fishing boats. An old man was splitting wood by hitting the back of an axe sunk into the log with a sledge.

I passed by Burnt Islands on the way down the coast. The sea was beautiful. Ponds were scattered across the hills. Some of the ponds cascaded into other ponds with rapids and waterfalls. Lots of gulls were on ponds and a flock of ducks too far away to identify crashed into a pond.

A large white bluff appeared in the distance. This was Diamond Cove. I drove down through the winding road to the end and finally found a place to turn around. A scenic cove with colored houses and boats—I wished for more time than a cursory look.

It is definitely exciting to drive up a hill seeing nothing but blue sky over the hood and find someone put a right-angle turn just over the top.

I passed the road to the coastal ferry that served coastal villages to Burgeo and villages and islands further south. The road to Harbour la Cou descended to sea level to a pretty village along a one-lane road. Remember the old folk song about Harbor la Cou? How about the Fellow from Fortune?

Finally getting turned around and extricating myself, I proceeded on to Rose Blanche and the granite Rose Blanche Lighthouse. Signs to the lighthouse led to the end of the paved road then pointed about another kilometer beyond the blacktop to the parking area with a B&B, shop and ticket office.

The walk to the lighthouse was along a hillside overlooking a rugged coast of coves, rocks and waves. No wonder they needed a lighthouse. This lighthouse was built in 1871 of native granite. It was decommissioned in the 1940s prior to confederation. The structure was restored beginning in 1996 using about 70% of the original material. The interior was redecorated as it might have been when the lighthouse keeper's family lived there. An operational light had recently been activated as a geographical landmark rather than a navigational site.

Vegetation included Royal Fern, Blackberries, Bunchberries, Heath, Prostrate Juniper, Blue Flags, Yarrow, Buttercup, Cow Parsnips, Hazel shrubs and brown grasses. A small flock of tiny birds disappeared into the Hazel.

There was a large rocky island off shore that the waves broke around and met on the shore side with a mean standing wave.

Rose Blanche was strung along the north shore of the cove with pretty houses and fishing boats. Returning from the lighthouse I drove through Rose Blanche and stopped for lunch. The road was a one-lane loop but at least it was marked as one-way.

After the scenic cruise of Rose Blanche I headed back towards Port-au-Basque. Burnt Islands and Isle aux Morts were seaward from the road and had a shipyard in addition to fishing.

I took the loop around the residential areas of Port-au-Basque and stopped at the mall. The museums were closed. At sunset I checked in at the ferry.

About 2300 we began to load the ferry. Busses and trucks drove on board first followed by cars. I paid for a dormitory bunk and took the blanket and pillow to my assigned space. As soon as we cleared the channel markers I crashed.

Day 22, 2 Oct 2003. I awoke about 0500 and went out on deck. Sydney, Nova Scotia, was visible on the horizon. We were in port and off loading by 0630. I followed the flow to the TCH 104.

The TCH followed the water but bypassed most of the little towns. About 0900 I crossed the causeway off of Cape Bretton. I stopped at a couple visitor information offices and found that they had closed for the season on 30 Sep.

A flight of a dozen Sandhill Cranes lifted off heading southwest

This piece of the TCH was two lanes with occasional passing lanes and paved shoulders. This looks like this was in anticipation of expansion someday. I passed Antigonish and New Glasgow and decided not to get in the way of hurricane recovery by not going to Prince Edwards Island.

I turned off on Hwy 102 towards Truro and the tidal bore and on to Halifax. The damage by Hurricane Juan had been mostly windburn and loss of leaves on the trees for the last 30km of TCH but at Truro there were some broken branches and trees that had been uprooted with the root ball. The motel near the tidal bore was still without electricity and the parking lot was full of branches. A lot of homes and building were still without electricity.

I looked at the bore on the Salmon River. It was 5 hours until the next event. A flock of Starlings fed in the grass and a bold Ringed-Bill Gull patrolled the picnic tables.

I went down stream to Clifton and Black Rock through some beautiful farm and dairy country. One barn was missing some of its roof. There were small areas where trees were broken or uprooted. This looked like microburst damage or some of the small satellite tornadoes. Fallen trees had damaged power lines, and repair vehicles blocked some of the roads. Most of the roads were passable with downed trees having been cut and pulled aside.

I took the back road, Provincial 2, to the Halifax airport. The road was one lane with repair crews in several places. Several locations on the Stubenacadie River were visible with the bore sculpting.

The information office in the airport said the airport hotel was closed. They found me housing in Truro for two nights and one night at a B&B in Enfield near the airport.

I spoke with the airport operations officer and wildlife manager. The airport had recovered. They were expecting some bird problems from earthworms and crickets brought up by the rain. I was really happy to see they were anticipating and planning instead of reacting.

Day 23, 3 Oct 2003. Kinda cool. It was about 8.

I called several numbers in Halifax to see if they needed volunteers for the clean up. I finally got through to a real person and was told to call the Salvation Army or the St Vincent DePaul Society. I called them and got answering machines.

I finally called the Red Cross in Truro and got hold of a real person. She said to come down about five and help deliver dinners. I arrived just before a group of touring political leaders including Premier Hamm of Nova Scotia, the Nova Scotia Member of Parliament, the local representative to the Nova Scotia parliament, the mayor and the chief of the Emergency Management Office. Their visit lasted about 15 minutes. After they left I joined another Red Cross volunteer to deliver several dinners to people without electricity.

The weather forecast showed possible frost overnight. Definitely time to head SOUTH. The weather also showed that Ft. McMurray and Yellowknife in Alberta were in the upper 20s

Day 24, 4 Oct 2003. TV said temperature was—1°C with 100% humidity. The car was coated with frost but this sublimed by 0900.

The other location recommended to view the tidal bore was Maitland near the mouth of the Shabenacadie R. I drove down the 30km and found several tours to ride the bore that were closed for the season or due to damage. The overlook at Maitland might be spectacular during tidal change but was a wide mud flat at low tide. A large flock of Starlings occupied the trees and ground.

I stopped at a couple of antique/craft shops that were mostly craft. No antiques of interest.

Tree damage was spotty. Most of the trees seemed to have been toppled by a SE wind. Many of the Spruce were broken as opposed to the oaks and maples that lay over complete with roots. This may be a function of being in full leaf. Along Rte 2 there were trees that had been across the road and on houses and a couple barns that had been damaged.

I found the B&B in Enfield just north of the airport and unloaded my bags. About 1300 I went to the airport to turn the car in. Almost 5800km.

About 1700 I rode along with the host to look at tree damage in Halifax and the area around Enfield. Not a lot of structural damage other than utilities but lots of big trees blown over. Many broken branches. The city park almost wiped out.

Premier Hamm announced that stores would be open Sunday for a one time only for hurricane relief.

This hurricane presented an excellent opportunity for the area to get an urban tree survey to identify hazard trees to be removed and good tree management plan to program tree replacement and urban forestry design. Many of the trees beneath power lines should be removed. Many of the street trees were mature and should have been scheduled for replacement. Infrastructure changes like putting the utilities underground should be programmed. Code changes should be made to include a list of preferred trees. Utility pruning should be routinely scheduled since some of the trees appeared not to have been pruned recently

Day 25, 5 Oct 2003. I was up at 0330 to get to the airport by 0430 to catch my plane at 0645. It had been overcast but began raining as the plane was loading. There were heavy clouds all the way to Newark. Temperature at Newark was 28° F. The flights to Memphis and San Antonio were uneventful. I was back home by 1530.

Observations and Recommendations.

There were several reasons for going to Nova Scotia and Newfoundland.

1. I had written several books on travel and history of Canada. I was looking for a Canadian publisher since there is not much market for

these subjects in Texas. During the trip I talked to several publishers in Halifax and St John's and found they would not publish non-Canadian authors. Catch 22.

2. I have written a number of travelogues punctuated with poetry. This trip would provide notes for another one on Newfoundland. I spent three weeks and drove almost 6000km in Nova Scotia and Newfoundland with lots of notes and over 400 pictures.

3. I was stationed at Argentia in 1960-61 and was curious to see how Newfoundland had changed over the past forty years. Observations of changes and my opinions are as follows:

    1. The visual impact seeing villages of colored buildings scattered along the shore is gone. The old colors seemed organic and blended into the environment. The new houses look more like beached icebergs and out of place. The character of the island has changed. The historic districts of St John's and the villages near Port-au-Basque are the only ones that have the old look.
    2. The painting of buildings was eliminated by installation of vinyl siding. I suggest that the energy people look at the difference in the solar energy absorption of white vinyl and the darker wood. There is a maintenance requirement for the vinyl that is largely ignored. There is fading and splitting of vinyl and a useful life of about 20 years. If a proper vapor barrier was not installed the house frame could deteriorate.
    3. I'm happy to say basic sanitation has really improved with regional water and sewage treatment and the elimination of outhouse, the chamber pot and the water bucket.
    4. Electrical and telephone and cable or satellite TV service are available almost universally. The drawback to this is the universal presence of transmission lines and power poles. Driving from St John's to Burin there is at least one transmission line in sight at all times.
    5. There are roads. When I arrived in 1960 TCH was mostly a gravel road. Most of the streams had low water crossing instead of bridges. The roads were almost seasonal since the spring thaw

turned them to knee-deep mud. Many villages were accessible only by boat or footpath.

6. There are vehicles. This has changed work and leisure patterns and improved education with busses and centralized schools. The evening promenade has largely disappeared with TV and the family car. Obesity has increased along with diabetes. I did see a number of women walking for exercise but few men.

7. Fishing has changed. Not only has the Cod and lobster yield decreased but the tackle and equipment had changed. Plastic jigs and lines and netting. Fiberglass boats with outboard motors replaced wooden dories, wooden boats and fifty-year-old two-cycle engines. I suggested applying fiberglass to the wooden hulls in 1961 but a priest in Grand Banks said if the fishermen did not have to build a new boat every winter they would just stay drunk.

8. In Mexico satellite TV is used to literally replace rural schools. There is classroom space and local supervision but large school complexes and teachers are not used like in the US and much of Canada. This might be the answer for smaller villages and the Southern Shore communities and reduce bussing instead of consolidating and centralizing the schools

Hurricane Juan has presented Halifax and Nova Scotia an excellent opportunity for urban planning and disaster preparedness. I had the opportunity to see Halifax on September 12-13 and Halifax, Truro and central Nova Scotia on 2-4 October after the hurricane. The city and Province should: A. Conduct an urban tree survey to map the tree, identify tree condition, identify hazard trees and prioritize removal for public safety and to reduce public liability; B. Prepare a good tree management plan to program tree to include urban forestry design a tree replacement plan; C. Many of the trees beneath power lines should be removed; D. Many of the street trees were mature and should have been scheduled for replacement; E. Most of the trees had been root pruned to install streets, curbs and sidewalks weakening the root ball; F. Infrastructure changes should be programmed such as putting the electrical, phone and TV cables underground; G. Municipal code changes should be made enforce the urban forestry plan to include a list of preferred trees; H. Utility pruning should be routinely scheduled since some of the trees appeared not to have been pruned recently

Invertebrates of Nova Scotia and Newfoundland (11 Sep-4 Oct 03)

Insects

Colias eurytheme	Orange Sulfur (Alfalfa Butterfly)
Pieris napi	Sharp-Veined White
Lambdina fiscellaria	Hemlock Looper

Land Snails

?	Slug
Capaea hortensis	Garden Snail

Barnacles

Semibalanus balanoides	Common Barnacle

Crabs

Cancer irroratus	Common Rock Crab
Hyas araneus	Toad Crab/Large Spider Crab

Mollusc

Littorina littorea	Common Periwinkle
Littorina saxatilus	Rough Periwinkle
Littorina obtusata	Smooth Periwinkle
Lunatia heros	Northern Moon Snail
Thais lapillus	Dog Whelk (Dog Winkle)
Buccinum undatum	Waved Whelk (Wrinkles)
Mytilus edulis	Blue Mussel
Placopecten magellanicus	Deep Sea Scallop
Ensis directus	Common Razor Clam
Mya arenaria	Soft Shelled Clam
Clinocardium cillatrum	Iceland Cockle (Fox Harbor)

Starfish

Asterias vulgaris	Northern Starfish/Purple Star/ Boreal Sea Star

Echinoderms

Stronglyocentrotus droebachiensis	Green Sea Urchin

Birds and Mammals of Nova Scotia and Newfoundland
(11 Sep-4 Oct 03)

Birds

Procellariidae-Shearwaters and Fulmars

Puffinus griseus	Sooty Shearwater	Open Atlantic Ocean

Hydrobatidae—Storm-Petrels

Oceanodroma leucohoa	Leach's Storm Petrel	Open Atlantic Ocean

Sulidae—Gannets

Moris bassana	Gannet	Coastal Atlantic Cape St Marys

Falconinae—Birds of Prey

Falco columbarius	Merlin	Cape St Marys NF

Buteoninae—Eagles

Haliaetus leucocephalus	Bald Eagle	NS

Phasianidae—Pheasants

Phasianus colchius	Ring-Necked Pheasant	NS

Gruidae—Cranes

Grus Canadensis	Sandhill Crane	NS

Charadriidae—Plovers

Charadrius semipalmatus	Semipalmated Sandpiper	NS

Laridae—Gulls and Terns

Larus delawarensis	Ring-Billed Gull	Coastal NS and NF
Larus argentatus	Herring Gull	Coastal NS and NF

Alcedinidae—Kingfishers

Megaceryle alcyon	Belted Kingfisher	NS

Tyrannidae—Flycatcher

Empidonax flaviventris	Yellow-Bellied Flycatcher	NF

Corvidae—Jays and Crows

Cyanocitta cristata	Blue Jay	Humber and Codroy Valleys NF
Perisoreus Canadensis	Gray Jay	Gros Morne Park NF
Corvus brachyrhynchos	American Crow	NS and NF

Paridae—Titmice

Parus atricapillus	Black-Capped Chickadee	Terra Nova Park NF

Turdidae—Old World Warblers and Thrushes

Turdus migratorius	American Robin	Northern Peninsula NF

Sturnidae—Starlings

<u>Sternus vulgarus</u>   Starling   Northern Peninsula NF

Parulidae—Warblers

<u>Dendroica striata</u>   Black-Poll Warbler   Terra Nova National Park

Fringillidae—Sparrows

<u>Zonotrichia albicollis</u>   White-throat Sparrow   NS and NF

Ploceidae—Weaver Finches

<u>Passer domesticus</u>   House or English Sparrow   Cowhead NF

Mammals

Raccoon
Porcupine   Roadkill   NS
Mink   Green Valley NF
Moose   Gros Morne
Eastern Chipmunk   Green Valley NF
Red Squirrel   NF, NS

Whales

<u>Megaptera novaelangliae</u>   Humpback Whale
<u>Balaenoptera physalus</u>   Finn Whale
<u>Balaenoptera acutorastrata</u>   Minke/Pothead Whale
<u>Lagenorhynchus albirostris</u>   White Beak Dolphin

Fish

<u>Mallotus villosus</u>   Capelins

Vegetation of Nova Scotia and Newfoundland
(11 Sep-4 Oct 03)

This is a listing of outstanding fall flowers and common plants but probably not all. Many of the plants are introduced and prefer disturbed grounds such as highway right-of-ways. The species seen are listed below.

Seaweeds

Chondrus crispus	Irish Moss	NS, NF
Fucus vesiculosus	Bladder Wrack	NS, NF
Fucus spiralis	Spiral Wrack	NS, NF

Lichens

Usnea sp.	Powdery Beard	NS, NF
?	Crustose lichens	NF
Cladina stellaris	Northern Reindeer Lichen	NF

Fungi

Aminita muscaria	Fly Agarica	NF
Lenzites betulina	Birch Maze-gill	NF

Selaginellaceae

Polytrichum piliferum	Awned Hair-cap	NF
Selaginella sp	NF	

11 Ferns

Matteuccia struthiopteris	Ostrich Fern	NS, NF

13 Pinaceae (Pine Family)

Abies balsamea	Balsam Fir	NF
Larix laricina	Larch	NF
Picea glauca	White Spruce	NF
Picea mariana	Black Spruce	NF, NS
Pinus strobus	White pine	NF, NS

15 Cupressaceae

Juniperus communis	Common or Prostrate Juniper	NF

17 Typhace

Typha latifolia	Common Cattail	NS, NF

18 Ginkoaceae

Ginko biloba	Ginko	NS

27 Gramineae (Grasses)

Calamagrostis Canadensis	Bluejoint Grass/Marsh Reed Grass	NF
Eriophorum sp.	Cotton Grass	NF

28 Cyperaceae

Carex sp	Sedges	NF
Eleocharis sp	Spikerushes	NF

42 Iridaceae

Iris versicolor	Blue Flag	NF
Iris Hookeri	Hooker's Iris	NF

48 Salicaceae

Populus tremuloides	Aspen	NS, NF

49 Myricaceae

Myrica gale	Sweetgale	NF

52 Betulaceae

Betula papyifera	birch	NS, NF
Betula pendula	White Birch	NS, NF
Corylus cornuta	hazel	NS, NF

62 Polygonaceae (Dock Family)

Rumex crispus	Curled Dock	NS, NF

72 Caryophyllaceae

Cerastium vulgatum	Mouse-Ear Chickweed	NS, NF
Stellaria media	Common Chickweed	NS, NF

73 Nymphaceae

Nymphacea ordorata	Fragrant water lily	NF

75 Ranunculaceae

Ranunculus acris	Common Anemones	NS, NF
Ranuncuus flammula	Spearwort	NF
Ranunculus repens	Creeping Buttercup	NF

84 Brassicaceae/Cruciferae (Mustard Family)

Brassica juncea	Chinese Mustard	NF
Cakile edentula	Sea-Rockets	NS, NF

94 Rosaceae (Rose Family)

Fragaria virginiana strawberries	NS, NF	
Fragaria sp. strawberries	NS, NF	
Potentilla fruticosa	Shrubby Cinquefoil	NF
Rubus chamaemorus	bakeapples	NS, NF
Rubus Idaeus	Red Raspberry	NS, NF
Rosa nitida	Northeastern Rose	NS, NF
Sanguisorba Canadensis	Canadian Bottlebrush	NS, NF
Spirea latifolia	Meadowsweet	NF

96 Fabiaceae/Leguminose (Bean Family)

Coronilla varia	Crown Vetch	NS
Lupinus polyphylus	Lupine	NS
Medicago sativa	alfalfa	NS, NF
Trifolium pratense	Red Clover	NS, NF
T. repen	White Clover	NS, NF
Vicia cracca	Cow Vetch	NS

99 Oxalidaceae

Oxalis sp.	Oxalis	NS, NF

113 Aceraceae (Maple Family)

<u>Acer</u> <u>rubrum</u>	Red Maple	NS

119 Tilliaceae

<u>Tilia</u> <u>vulgaris</u>	Linden trees	NS

131 Labiate (Mint Family)

<u>Prunella</u> <u>vulgaris</u>	Selfheal	NS, NF

138 Onagraceae

<u>Epilobium</u> <u>angustifolium</u>	Fireweed	NF
<u>Oenothera</u> <u>parviflora</u>	Small Flowered Evening Primrose	NF
<u>Oenothera</u> <u>perennis</u>	Sundrops	NF

141 Apiaceae (Umbelliferae)

<u>Daucas</u> <u>carota</u>	Queen Anne's Lace	NS, NF
<u>Heracleum</u> <u>maximum</u>	Cow Parsnip	NF

142 Cornaceae

<u>Cornus</u> <u>canidensis</u>	Bunchberry/ Crackerberry	NS, NF

144 Ericaceae

<u>Calluna</u> <u>vulgaris</u>	heather	NF
<u>Empetrum</u> <u>nigrum</u>	Black Crowberry	NF
<u>Gaultheria</u> <u>hispidula</u>	creeping snowberry	NF
<u>Kalmia</u> <u>angustifoliua</u>	Sheep Laurel	NF
<u>Ledum</u> <u>groenlandicum</u>	Labrador Tea	NF
<u>Vaccinium</u> <u>angustifolium</u>	blueberries	NF
<u>Vaccinium</u> <u>vitis-idaea</u>	cranberries	NF

165 Scrophulariaceae (Figwort Family)

Euphrasia sp.	Eyebright	NS, NF
Linaria vulgari	Butter-and-eggs	NS, NF

172 Plantaginaceae

Plantago major	Dooryard Plantain	NS, NF

173 Rubiaceae

Hedyotis caerulea	Bluets	NF

178 Campanulaceae

Campanula rotundifolia	Harebell	NF

180 Compositae (Daisy Family)

Achillea millefolium	Yarrow	NS, NF
Anaphalis margaritacea	Pearly Everlasting	NS, NF
Aster novae-belgii	New York Aster	NS, NF
Centaurea nigra	Black Knapweed	NS
Chrysanthemum leucanthemum	Chrysanthemum	NF
Cirsium arvense	Canada Thistle	NF
Cirsium muticum	Swamp Thistle	NF
Eupatorium maculatum	Joe-Pye Weed	NS, NF
Leontodon autmnalis	Fall Dandelion	NS, NF
Solidago sp.	Goldenrod	NS, NF
Tussilago farfara	Colts Foot	NF

Do Bears Do It In the Woods?

A Week in Winnipeg and Riding Mountain National Park, Manitoba, Canada

Contents

Do Bears Do It In the Woods?

My wife, Carol, and I were off for a week to Winnipeg and Riding Mountain National Park in the Province of Manitoba, Canada. I was looking forward to sub-Arctic in the summer and the summer solstice on the shore of Lake Winnipeg. Who knows? There should be moose, giant mosquitoes and black flies, sunny wheat fields, and prairie potholes full of waterfowl. Maybe I'd even find the answer to the old question, "Do bears do it in the woods?"

Winnipeg

A taxi arrived a 0500 on **Thursday 10 June 1993**. It took us to the airport for a 0630 Northwest Airline flight to Memphis, TN, and the first leg of our trip. The flight was 25 minutes late leaving San Antonio so we lost our seats to Minneapolis for the next leg. We each received $100 credit on future flights and seats on the next flight at 1000 that would still arrive in time for our connection to Winnipeg. This flight was 45 minutes late and we just made the Winnipeg flight at 1310.

At Winnipeg there was no trouble with immigration, the rental car or our reservations at the Quality Inn.

We drove downtown and arrived at the hotel at 1600. This Quality Inn was a disaster. Apparently it had just been purchased by the Quality Inn hotel chain and had been a second rate hotel. There were cheap towels and no soap; the rooms and elevator smelled of disinfectant; the carpet was threadbare; and the restaurant and bar were permanently closed. I called the Delta Winnipeg and got a reservation beginning the next morning. The Delta, a 4-star hotel, had a weekend special cheaper than the Quality Inn.

Carol rested while I walked three blocks to the Hudson Bay Company (HBC) Archives. They were just closing at 1630 so I spent a half-hour in the Winnipeg Museum of Art until their closing time. I went across the street and wandered through the HBC main store. This large, two-block square, six-story department store had a small town attitude about displays. HBC sold everything from antiques and Arctic art to VCRs and designer clothing to wood stoves. HBC even had a discount outlet in the basement.

It rained more than an inch in the hour I was in the store. The drainage system was so efficient that an hour later you could hardly tell it had rained. The temperature was about 20ºC (68ºF) with a low expected of about 6ºC (43ºF). The western provinces had been so wet and cool. The spring fruit crop had been destroyed, the summer crops were late and birds were returning late.

We moved early Friday morning, then went out for breakfast at a huge downtown mall. We each had big sweet roll, an egg and sausage croissant and hot chocolate at one of the coffee shops. Several locals noticed we were from out of town and we had an interesting discussion of local history, real estate prices, jobs, taxes and changes in Winnipeg in the past few years.

I spent the afternoon in the HBC Archives while Carol went to the Forks Park Mall where the Assinibonne River runs into the Red River. I found several articles on the time period when Uncle Otto was in the Yukon in 1898 and several references to people he had noted in his diary. There were no pictures or official records of the steamboat, *Enterprise*, that he built, taken to the Arctic, and finally sold to the HBC.

We met back in the hotel about 1700 and went to Chinatown for supper at the Kum Koon Dim Sum restaurant. The Dim Sum selection was very good.

Our room at the Delta Winnipeg was on the 12th floor. Picture windows looked south half way to the US border. Flat land and grain elevators could be seen to the east, south and west. At night few lights showed beyond the lights of metropolitan Winnipeg.

Lake Winnipeg

On Saturday, June 12, we took a self-guiding driving tour suggested in one of the guidebooks. Beginning in downtown Winnipeg the first leg was up Main St. through Chinatown. We continued north past several parks and a municipal golf course till we met Perimeter Highway 101. The road went east and crossed the Red River finally intersecting Provincial Highway 59. Driving north we passed Birds Hill Provincial Park and finally intersected Hwy. 44.

About four miles east on Hwy 44 we turned south on Hwy 306 to visit Cooks Creek. This farming community had a Russian Orthodox Church, the Church of Immaculate Conception, with the Grotto of Our Lady of Lourdes. The small Cooks Creek museum was not yet open for the summer, which officially began on 1 July. Most of the houses were well back from the road and had pine and spruce tree windbreaks planted on all sides. Most of them had large vegetable gardens and tall, elegantly shaped martin houses. Numerous bluebird houses perched on top of fence posts a hundred feet apart.

Returning to Hwy. 44, we continued east towards the town of Beausejour. I stopped along the road at a quarry to look at the dolomite limestone and the fossils. We dropped in at a garage sale to look and talk to the people. Their garden was in and the peas and beans and squash were just coming up.

At Beausejour we stopped at a bank to purchase some Canadian dollars. This modern brick Bank of Canada branch had a pleasant human teller. She mentioned that we should visit the Broken-Beau Historical Museum but that it was not yet open for the summer.

Leaving Beausejour, Hwy. 44 continued east through the Agassiz Provincial Forest. The "forest" was not quite what I had expect—second growth spruce and hemlock not more that twenty years old.

We turned north on Hwy. 11. The first feature along this road was the Seven Sisters Falls hydroelectric plant, the largest of the six dams and power plants on the Winnipeg River. The power plants generate power from low dams that had replaced the original rapids.

The second growth timber was interspersed with marshy fields and pastures. Many of fields we passed sprouted numerous goose blinds. The geese had not yet begun to arrive from the south.

Lac du Bonnet on the Winnipeg River was the first town of any size. We drove through a nicely developed residential area along the Winnipeg River and through the small downtown area. The number of motels and rental offices indicated a large tourist population during the fishing season. Walleye fishing was the big sport and commercial mainstay. The female Walleyes were still spawning so the fishing season was not open yet.

It was noon and lunchtime. We had a choice of the only restaurant open this time of year or the Chicken Shack. The restaurant did not serve walleye because it had to be government inspected. Their special was fried chicken. We had their special and a special order of ice for Carol's coke.

Roads turned off to McArthur Falls and Great Falls dams and power plants, which we passed. We took a road to look at Mud Falls, one of two falls on the river that had not been dammed and stopped along the river to take pictures.

The Winnipeg River was a half mile wide with a rocky shoreline and a large sand bar island in mid stream. There was a grassy mud flat below the island that came and went as the water level changed with the power plant discharges.

A lady with a dog came out to see what we were up to. She and her husband had a cottage next to her parent's home and spent most of their weekends on the river. They were Billie and Karl Karlson and they ran a contracting company in Winnipeg. We talked to them for a couple hours and promised we would be back the next Saturday for the solstice.

The next stop was at Pine Falls and the Abitibi Paper Company. This was the first and largest paper mill in Manitoba. It emitted the typical rotten egg odor of paper plants but had not seriously impacted the river. I guess this was where the forest had gone.

Five miles further down river was the site of Fort Alexander, a HBC trading post established in 1792. It became an important site in the bitter land battles of the next century.

An Indian Reservation occupied both sides of the road for the next several miles. The houses were less substantial than the private homes outside the reservation. There was no farming. Several people had said they would gladly take our Blacks if we would take their Indians.

We passed from the Prairie Vegetative Province to the Subarctic Province. With a remarkable change in vegetation, the spruce forest began.

At the junction of Hwy 12 we went north to Victoria Beach. This was largely a weekend residential area with no public access to the lake. We headed south to Grand Beach and stopped for a look at the lake and the fine white sand beaches. There were few clamshells and some driftwood. The lake was calm and you could see the other shore on the horizon about 15 miles away from atop the dunes.

Evening was falling as we headed down Hwy 59 to Selkirk and Lockport to Winnipeg. Back at the hotel we made reservations for Mother Tuckers restaurant for 2030. This first class restaurant was about three blocks from the hotel. The prime rib was very good and the service was above average for anywhere.

Riding Mountain

Shortly after sun up on Sunday morning we checked out and began the three-hour drive to Riding Mountain National Park. The temperature was about 8°C as we stopped by Forks Park for breakfast. They were having a run for charity along the river and had clowns and a local DJ. The mall contained a number of interesting shops and eating-places.

About 1000 we left Forks Park to go to the Fort Whyte Center for Environmental Education on McCreary Road. Part of the road near the Center was not-very-good dirt and not well marked. This abandoned gravel quarry had several borrow pits converted for fishing and waterfowl lakes. Volunteers staffed a small natural history museum. We hiked the self-guiding nature walk under a cool overcast. Hundreds of Yellow-headed Blackbirds and Red-wing Blackbirds were in the cattails; Canadian Geese, Franklin Gulls, Mallards and a Killdeer were on or near the open water; and a Bay-breasted Warbler and a Black-headed Grosbeak were in the trees near a clearing with bird feeders. The arctic toad (<u>Bufo</u> <u>borias)</u> and spring peepers were calling around the lakes.

Drizzle began to fall as we drove out McGillivray Blvd. to Perimeter Hwy 101 and then north to Canada 1, the Trans Canada Highway. Gas was $.51 per liter when we filled up and headed west for Portage la Prairie. The weather was cool and misty all the way.

The land was flat and lightly wooded to Portage. Rolling hills undulated to the west along Hwy 16 towards Minnedosa. The area around Minnedosa was hilly and deeply marked with glacial scars. We turned north on Highway 10 through green hills peppered with s mall glacial ponds called prairie potholes.

Near Erickson the escarpment on which Riding Mountain Park was located became the dominant feature on the horizon. From Onanole to Wasagaming the road was lined with tourist resorts and trailer parks.

Our condo was about three miles north of Wasagaming. It had a pool, gym, golf course, meeting rooms and a stable. The village of Wasagaming was built around the Riding Mountain National Park headquarters. The village had several restaurants and numerous motels and private cabins. There was one grocery and a gas station but no bank.

On Monday morning we visited the park visitor center and bought our park permit. The visitor center had interpretive displays, a gift shop and a picnic area. We picked up a few groceries and had lunch at one of the restaurants. The special was perogies—a Ukrainian pastry shell containing potatoes and cabbage.

We drove along a park road leading to Lake Audy and the buffalo enclosures. The buffalo were still in winter pasture. Robins and crows were plentiful. Cliff swallows were building nests under the eves of the viewing area. Morning dove and Rock Doves were present in limited numbers. It was still too cool for most birds.

On the way back to the condo we stopped at a fruit stand for some fresh "Canadian" fruit. The cool, wet spring had set back or ruined much of the local crop so our plums and apricots were fresh from California.

About 1800 we hiked the Loon's Island trail on the east end of Katherine Lake. It was 2.4 KM or about 1.5 miles. The trail started with a view of the lake and lead through a meadow and aspen with a thick growth of hazel. Robins were abundant. About a half-hour's walk and we were out on the lakes shore.

A pair of Loons was swimming on the lake and we heard a couple Loon calls. A young eagle flew over as we were leaving the lake. White and yellow sweet clover, pepperwort and chickweed flowered in the sun. Marsh Marigold, white and purple violets and anemone bloomed in the shade.

We stopped near a pond along the highway and watched a beaver swimming across the pond. He saw us. He slapped his tail on the water's surface and disappeared.

Light gradually faded until almost 2300. The night sky was black with twinkling stars. We were right under the Big Dipper and 1500 miles north of San Antonio.

The night sky slowly yielded to dawn. About 0500 it was light at a cool 6ºC (42ºF).

About 1000 Tuesday we walked the Arrowhead Trail. This was 3.4 KM or about 2 miles. It began in an old meadow that was being taken over by willow and aspen. The trail dropped into a dense black spruce forest that cut out the light to anything else. It was moist but bare under the spruce trees.

A depression lake, locally called a "kettle", announced itself with calling toads and frogs. A short side trail led to Pudge Lake where a loon was swimming in the distance. There were several beaver runs used to haul branches to the lake. A large beaver lodge emerged about fifty feet off shore.

Many small Blues, butterflies less than an inch across the wings, flew along the trails. They flitted with dizzying speed in the open woods. They landed and almost disappeared into the litter of the trail not allowing an approach of closer than six feet. They belonged to the Lyaenidae family of butterflies with the Hair-streaks and Coppers and are probably the most numerous and common family in the Arctic.

Out of the woods we returned to Wasagaming to look for a bank. We found we would have to go to Erickson.

Erickson was a small town about twenty miles south of the park with a public school still in session. There were two banks and three restaurants and a farmer's co-op grocery. We had lunch and then bought groceries. At the western end of the main street was a Viking long boat, a monument to the town's Scandinavian heritage.

We returned to the condo and I took the Brule or "burnt" trail alone. Brule trail was 4.2 KM to Kinosoa Lake returning by a parallel trail. The walk proceeded through a burned out forest, which had been ignited by lightning. The area was recovering and a grove of aspen was taking over the site. This grove was all from root sprouts or basically one tree. The trail then went through a mixed wood with aspen, jack pine and white spruce. Dwarf mistletoe or "witches broom" occurred on many of the conifers. An ongoing research program was looking for a control for this parasite. Black spruce was the only thing growing in the low spots and the ground felt spongy with fallen leaves. Jack pine and white spruce occupied the ridges. The trail ended on a boardwalk across a bog. The bog supported marsh marigold, Labrador tea, short thin horsetails and many other hydrophytic plants. Lake Kinosao had clear brown water and swarms of mosquitoes. Several small tamarack trees grew out of the bog.

The alternate trail back showed several moose tracks and a bear print coming my way. Bearberry or kinnikinik was in bloom. A grove of aspen had bear marks on several of the trees. Black bears ripped long gashes in the bark as they climbed the trees in early spring to eat the catkins. I stepped over a fallen log and found more bear tracks and a fresh pile of green bear excreta.

The trail ended in a clearing with scattered willow and birch thickets. Blue-eyed-grass and one of the prairie fescues dominated the clearing but several Spotted Coralroot Orchids were in bloom. I got back to the condo about 2030.

DO BEARS DO IT IN THE WOODS?

In an aspen grove
in Canada
in June

Bear tracks.
Toes pointing towards me.
We didn't meet.

Aspen trees with bear marks.
A hungry bear had climbed to eat
a just-woke-up salad of aspen catkins

Stepping over a fallen log
I find a huge pile of odorless, green
bear dung.

I have finally discovered
the answer-
yes!

*   *   *

Wednesday, 16 June, began at a crisp and foggy at 6ºC (42ºF). We left early and drove 15 miles north to walk the Boreal Island trail at dawn. On the way a large whitetail deer and an elk cow and calf were seen in along the right-of-way. Near the end of the divided highway single large coyote was just walking along. We turned around and came back and there he was, posing. After we had shot several pictures he came right up to the car like this was a regular thing to him.

The 1-km walk along the Boreal Island trail was interesting. A well-documented self-guiding trail passed through grassland, a creek bottom with aspen and spruce woods. This walk took about an hour.

It was about 1000 and we decided to see the town of Dauphin. It was a few miles north, outside the park. Dauphin's visitor's bureau offered a self-guiding tour of the town so we saw the highlights of town. Dauphin, on the Vermilion River, had about 8500 inhabitants. They had a statue of an Amisk (beaver in the Cree Indian language). We looked at a nice residential section, several old churches and several grain elevators.

It seems that almost every town and many villages in Manitoba had a historical museum and/or art museum and a well-manned visitor center. This appears to be an important indicator of the vitality of the area. Here, Fort Dauphin had been converted into a local historical museum with a large collection of photographs and artifacts, and an archeological display. Several types of buildings had been moved in and furnished with period material—a trapper's cabin, two log cabins, a school house, and a blacksmith shop. A fur trader rendezvous is scheduled in September each year.

Lunch was of Ukrainian food consisting of cabbage rolls, perohka (similar to empanadas but with potato stuffing) and link sausage. They did not have ice for Carols Coke.

The last stop on tour of Dauphin was the Dr. Vernon L. Watson Arts Center. Located in Dr Watson's restored circa 1905 house, the exhibits were works of several talented young local artists along with some of their permanent collection. A discussion with the curator indicated the presence of an active art community for a town of 8500.

On the way back the condo we saw a tour bus parked on the shoulder. The driver was trying to get a black bear to pose so we took several pictures too. We also stopped at a pond and watched beavers and a horned grebe with young.

Thursday, 17 Jun, began clear and cool at 8ºC (46ºF). About 1000 we drove east on Highway 19 through an area that had been burned a few years previous. A thick uniform growth of trees with a few standing burned snags was home to a lot of cottontail rabbits.

We hiked the Burls and Bittersweet trail, 2.2-km on the eastern edge of the escarpment. A hardwood forest community predominated. The eastern exposure to the sun and the protection from the north wind put flowering vegetation a couple weeks ahead of the rest of the park. The trail paralleled Dead Ox Creek with its broken shale bed. Several berries and two orchids—Lady's-slipper and Coralroot—were in bloom.

We left the park again and went east to the village of McCreary and the Mount Agassiz ski area. The land was gently rolling with the Riding Mountain escarpment looming in the west. About 600 year around residents maintained the ski area and motels and did some farming. McCreary had an airport and bus terminal, a nice library and an active Arts Council. We stopped at the only restaurant for lunch. Their special—fried chicken.

On the way back from McCreary Carol dropped me at the beginning of the Gorge Creek trail. This was a 6-km trail and she would pick me up in three hours. The trail dropped 1000 feet over the escarpment. I got off to a bad start on an unmarked side trail. The hike went literally down hill several hundred feet to the creek. Between the steep slope and mud, it was impossible to climb back up. This was interesting hiking stepping from rock to rock down the creek bed or following game trails along the side. There were bear signs and elk and deer signs. The cool shade hid patches of moss, liverworts and horsetails. After about a Km and two hours I climbed up the slope following game trails to the top and then broke through 200M of beaked hazel thicket to the road. The hazel thicket was neatly cropped by moose at about 4-5 feet, just short enough for me to see over.

Back on the road, I started walking the remaining 4-km to my pickup point. As I rounded a bend in the road a black bear was crossing the road about 200m ahead of me. It disappeared into the woods but I started kicking gravel and singing to scare anything that might be in the woods. My wife said it was a wonder that I didn't scare the trees, too. About a kilometer along the road a Park Ranger and his wife picked me up. They lived just east of the park and had frequent bear visits. Carol roared past and we tried to wave her down. She kept on so they took me to the trail end to meet her.

Friday, 18 June. It was light about 0430 since the sun only had to cross about 120 degrees of the horizon. It was 4ºC. About 0900 we went to Wasagaming and the visitors center then south through Erickson and Minnedosa to Brandon.

Brandon was an agricultural town of about 40,000 and the second largest city in Manitoba. One of the principle industries was the Agriculture Canada Research Station. They were famous for research in cattle and swine breeding, soil management and cereal grain research. Brandon hosted the Art Gallery of Southwestern Manitoba. Their current exhibition was a display of modern photographic montages. We drove past Brandon University with its collection of turn of the century and modern buildings. After lunch we hit several used bookstores and returned to the park.

Our chalet-style cabin at the Elkhorn Lodge was comfortable. It consisted of a bedroom, a bath and a kitchen/living room with satellite TV and a fireplace downstairs. There were two small bedrooms upstairs. The two TV channels, from Brandon and Winnipeg, faded in and out. We packed up and checked out so we could leave early.

Saturday, 19 June was here already. We were up at 0500 and it was already light. The car was loaded and we went north to Hwy 19 and headed east. There were rabbits in groups of two or three along the road through the second growth timber of the burned out area. From the edge of the escarpment Lake Manitoba was gleaming in the sun. A sage hen and chicks crossed the road in slow motion and finally disappeared into the vegetation at the roadside. Highway 5 headed south through the towns of Riding Mountain, Nepewa and Carberry to the TCH and east arriving in Winnipeg about 1000.

Two hours shopping in the Hudson Bay Company store found items like wood stoves and snowmobiles and Inuit art but nothing we couldn't resist.

After lunch of honeyed chicken livers at a Chinese restaurant we headed for Great Falls and the Karlsons. We had a pleasant afternoon and evening for the summer solstice. Karl had a line set fishing for walleye.

One about 18 inches hit and was landed. When it was released a gull made several grabs for it. The fish escaped.

Karl's sons went out to a sandbar in the middle of the river and brought back about 40 clams, which were cooked, into a stew. The six-month-old granddaughter had a liver cyst that had to be removed but the kid was a lively little girl. (The operation, a couple weeks later, was a complete success.)

On Sunday, 20 June, the sunset had been outstanding down the river and, after a night in a camp trailer, the sunup up river at 0515 was too.

WINNIPEG RIVER: SOLSTICE SUNRISE

On the Winnipeg River
it was light at four AM.
The horizon was broken with trees.
The sun rose at Oh Five Ten
ushered in by a swift, cool breeze.

Half the river was a mirror
that reflected the rising sun.
The other half was covered with ripples,
the breeze was having fun.

Herring gulls called.
The breeze disappeared.
The sky turned pink
then yellow
then blue.
The longest day of the year had dawned.
Half the solar year was through.

* * *

Homeward Bound

After breakfast and farewells we left about 0900 arriving in Winnipeg about noon.

The plane was on time but the connecting flight out of Minneapolis was an hour late so the plane in Memphis was already pulling out when we arrived at the gate.

MISSED OPPORTUNITY

We taxied north at Memphis
on Northwest flight 1161.
A red sun set behind blue clouds,
summer solstice eve was done.

If we had taken off just minutes before
we might have seen the sun rise in the west
but at the end of a long hard day
just one sunrise and sunset in a day is best.

—

We were home by 2200.

Carl Lahser 930630

PLANTS OF RIDING MOUNTAIN NATIONAL PARK MANITOBA, CANADA

14-19 JUNE 1993

Legend.
Arrowhead = A,
Brule = B,
Gorge Creek = C,
Burls and Bittersweet = D,
Moon Lake = E.,
Boreal Island = F.
Loon's Island = L,
** denotes plant in bloom

Ref: 1. *Plants of Riding Mountain National Park, Manitoba.* Agriculture Canada Pub. 1818/E. 1988.

2. *List of Vascular Plants of Riding Mountain National Park.* Parks Canada. 1977.
3. *Alaska Trees and Shrubs.* USDA Agriculture Handbook No. 410. Wash D.C. 1972.
4. *Wildflowers Across the Prairies.* F.R. Vance, J. R. Jowsey and J. S. McLean. Douglas and McIntyre. Vancouver. 1984.

Common Name	
Generic Name	Location

Lycopodiaceae
1. Stiff Club Moss

Lycopodium annotium L.   C

2. Club moss

L. dendroideum Michx.   C

Selaginellaceae
3. Selaginella

Selaginella selaginoides (L) Link   B

Equisetaceae
4. Field horsetail

Equisetum arvense L.   B, C

5. Swamp Horsetail

E. fluviatile L.   C

6. Common Scouring Rush

E. hymenale L.   C

7. Marsh horsetail

E. palustre L.   L

8. Meadow Horsetail

E. pratense Ehrh.   D

9. Dwarf Scouring Rush

E. scirpiodes Michx.   L

Pinaceae
10. Balsam Fir
<u>Abies balsamea</u> (L.) Mill.   B
11. Tamarax
<u>Larix laricina</u> (du Roi) K. Koch.   B
12. White spruce <u>Picea glauca</u> (Moech) Voss   all
13. Black Spruce
<u>P. mariana</u> (Mill) BSP   all
14. Jack Pine
<u>Pinus banksiana</u> Lamb.   B

Typhaceae
15. Common Cattail
<u>Typha latifolia</u> L.   all

Alismataceae
16. Western Water-plantain **
<u>Alisma triviale</u> Pursh   A

Liliaceae
17. Nodding Trillium **
<u>Trillium cernum</u> L.   D

Iridaceae
18. Blue-eyed-grass **
<u>Sisyrinchium montanum</u> Greene   B

Orchidaceae
19. Spotted Coralroot Orchid **
 <u>Corallorhiza maculata</u> Raf.   B
20. Yellow Lady's-slipper **
<u>Cypripedium calceolus</u> L.   D
21. Round-leaved orchid **

Orchis rotundifolia Banks   B, D

Salicaceae
22. Balsam Poplar
Populus balsamifera L.   B

Betulaceae
23. Speckled Alder
Alnus rugosa (DuRoi) Clausen   C

Fagaceae
24. Bur Oak
Quercus macrocarpa Michx.   D, F

Ulmaceae
25. American Elm
Ulmus americana L.   D

Caryophyllaceae
26. Field Chickweed **
Cerastium arvense L.   all

27. Long-stalked Chickweed **
Stellaria longipes Goldie.   B
28. Common Chickweed **
S. media (L) Cyril.   B

Ranunculaceae
29. Red Baneberry **
Actaea rubra (Ait) Willd.   D
30. Wild Columbine **
Aquilegia canadensis L.   D
31. Marsh Marigold **

<u>Caltha palustris</u> L.   all
32. Prairie buttercup
<u>Ranunculus rhomboideus</u> Goldie.   B

<u>Brassicaceae (Cruciferae)</u>
33. Common Peppergrass **
<u>Lepidium densiflorum</u> Schrad.   D

<u>Rosaceae</u>
34. Saskatoon-berry **
<u>Amelanchier alnifolia</u> Nutt.   D
35. Wild Strawberry **
<u>Fragaria virginiana</u> Dene.   all
36. Three-flowered Avens **
<u>Geum triflorum</u> Pursh   B
37. Shrubby Cinquefoil **
<u>Potentilla fruticosa</u> L.   D
38. Pin Cherry **
<u>Prunus pensynvanica</u> L.   D
39. Choke Cherry **
<u>P.virginiana</u> L.   D
40. Low Prairie Rose **
<u>Rosa arkansana</u> Porter   all
41. Common Wild Rose **
<u>R. woodsii</u> Lindl.   all

<u>Fabaceae (Leguminosae)</u>
42. Wild Peavine **
<u>Lathyrus venosus</u> Muhl.   D
43. White Sweet Clover **
<u>Melilotis alba</u> Desr.   all
44. Yellow Sweet Clover **
<u>M. officinalis</u> (L) Lam.   all

Anacardiaceae
45. Poison-Ivy
<u>Rhus radicans</u> L.   all

Violaceae
46. Early blue violet **
<u>Viola adunca</u> J.E. Smith   all

Araliaceae
47. Wild Sasparilla **
<u>Aralia nudicaulis</u> L.   D

Cornaceae
48. Bunchberry **
<u>Cornus canadensis</u> L.   D

Pyrolaceae
49. Common Pink Wintergreen **
<u>Pyrola asarifolia</u> Michx.   A

Eriaceae
50. Common Bearberry **
<u>Arctostaphylos uva-ursi</u> (L) Spreng   B
51. Labrador Tea **
<u>Ledum groenlandicum</u> Oeder   B

Boraginaceae
52. Horry Puccoon **
<u>Lithospermum canescens</u> (Michx)Lehm   all
53. Tall Lungwort **
<u>Mertensia paniculata</u> (Ait) G. Don   all

Scrophulariceae
54. Common Lousewort
<u>Pedicularis canadensis</u> Michx.   F

Rubiaceae
55. Northern Bedstraw **
<u>Galium boreale</u> L.   D
56. Long-leaved Bluet **
<u>Houstinia longifolia</u> Gaertn.   A

Caprifoliaceae
57. Twining Honeysuckle **
<u>Lornicera dioica</u> L.   all
58. Nannyberry **
<u>Viburnum lentago</u> L.   D
59. High Bush Cranberry **
<u>V. trilobum</u> Marsh   D

Asteraceae (Compositae)
60. Common Dandelion
<u>Taraxicum officinale</u> Weber.   all

O BEARS DO IT IN THE WOODS?

In an aspen grove
in Canada
in June

Bear tracks.
Toes pointing towards me.
We didn't meet.

Aspen trees with bear marks.
A hungry bear had climbed
to eat a just-woke-up salad
of aspen flowers.

Stepping over a fallen log
I find a huge pile of
odorless,
green
bear dung.

I have finally discovered
the answer-
yes!

Bird Strike
Conference 2005

14-25 Aug 05

Contents

Vancouver, Victoria, and the Inside Passage
14-25 Aug 05

Bird Strike 2005 was scheduled for 15-18 August, 2005, in Vancouver, British Columbia. This was a conference to discuss the latest developments in keeping birds and airplanes separated. I wanted to see who was still in the field, what was new, and to look for possible work. I had attended the BASH meeting here in 1998.

My wife, Carol, wanted to come along to Vancouver so we decided to expand the trip to include a trip to Victoria, then up to Port Hardy, and a round trip up the Inside Passage to Prince Rupert on the BC Ferry, *Queen of the North*.

The least expensive transportation we found was on Southwest Airlines from San Antonio to Seattle and return. We booked a bus trip from Seattle to Vancouver and a ferry trip from Victoria to Seattle.

Seattle, Vancouver, and Victoria are all major historic sites with a long and rich history. Fur trading, fishing, gold rushes, mining, shipping, railroads are right there along with plagues of small pox, swindling the aboriginals, disenfranchising the Chinese population, and political intrigues. The weather is generally mild and agriculture flourishes. Population, wages, real estate costs, and crime are rapidly rising.

August 14th

A taxi took us to the airport at 0500 to arrive two hours early for a 0710 flight. However, the ticket counter did not open until 0540. The flight got off ten minutes late into an overcast sky. We arrived in Phoenix on time with the weather looking like it would rain. The Phoenix area was green as a result of the monsoon rains of the previous month. Takeoff was delayed 20 minutes but we made up fifteen minutes and arrived in Seattle only 5 minutes late. Seattle weather was cool and clear and the snow-covered mountains were spectacular.

We had an hour to wait for the bus to Vancouver. The bus left the airport at 1530 and stopped in downtown Seattle below the Space Needle for more passengers. Leaving we passed a place with a couple of WWII amphibious DUWKs for harbor rides.

The plastic windows of the bus were flexible and a distorted mess not suited for photography so no Seattle pictures.

Trees along US1 were mostly conifers with occasional False Acacia (Robinia) and other broad leaf trees like Mountain Ash (Sorbus scopulina) with its bunches of red-orange fruit. There were bunches of Lady Fern (Althyrium filix-femina) but most of the grass in the median was brown. There were a few Madrones (Arbutus menzeii) and a number of dead spruce trees probably from budworm.

A '59 Buick convertible floated by on US 1 heading north.

All of the sycamore trees appear to have anthracnose.

We picked up a few more passengers at the Everett AMTRAC station. A commuter train called the Sounder was sitting in the station probably waiting for tomorrow's crowd.

Few flowers were in bloom. I saw patches of bloomed out Fireweed (Epilobium angustifolium) and patches of blackberries (Rubus sp). One field had a patch of Perennial Sow Thistle (Sonchus arvensis). Cattails (Typha latifolia) that had already shed the female flowers were growing in wet swales along the highway.

There were several Western Meadowlarks (Sternella neglecta) perched on the power lines and a flock of sparrows of some kind dashed out of a tree and into an abandoned brown field.

We made a short stop for Canadian customs and immigration at the border. Common Plantain (Plantago major), Ribwort Plantain (Plantago lanceolata), and Common Dandilion (Taraxicum officinalis) were growing in pavement joints.

Across the border in Canada were several more small flocks of sparrows and a few starlings and crows.

A large greenhouse operation was for sale or lease. There were fields of potatoes, cabbage, half grown corn, Vidalia onions, and herds of cattle and flocks of sheep.

Vancouver came into view with lots of grain elevators. We passed a Tim Horton so we were officially in Canada. About half of the population of British Columbia lives around Vancouver.

The bus arrived at the Vancouver airport about 1930. We got our bags and caught shuttle to the Richmond Hotel and Convention Center. Six years ago this was a couple of miles from the bus line but now it was right down town sharing a parking lot with the Marriott.

Wow. A 7th floor room with a balcony and a good view. Could hardly believe it. We went down for supper about 2100. The restaurant in our hotel was closing so we went next door to the Marriott. Nothing to rave about. Less than 4 ounces of halibut for $21C.

Sunset

August 15ᵗʰ

Monday began by waking up at 0430 local time. I finally got up about 0700. It was clear and 18°C. out on the balcony. The hotel buffet was $12.95 so I went across the street for $6 pancakes.

I registered for the conference about 0830 and sat through the presentations while Carol took the bus down town.

Monday evening was a reception. A number of old acquaintances were present. I talked to Ron Merritt and discussed doing my BASH play at the BBQ Tuesday night.

August 16ᵗʰ

Tuesday morning was overcast and 18°C. It had rained during the night and Whistler and the other mountains to the north were lost in fog. I went to the meeting while Carol went to the hairdresser.

Disappearing Whistler

Last night Whistler Mountain
Stood out over Vancouver.
Silhouetted against the twilight sky
Dawn broke to the tinkle of raindrops
Whistler and Vancouver were gone.

* * *

There was an afternoon field trip to the George C. Reifel Migratory Bird Sanctuary on Westham Island Tuesday afternoon. The refuge was near the town of Ladner. It had been the Reifel family farm where they had produced sugar beet seeds for WWII. They converted it to a bird sanctuary in the 1960s. The busses left the hotel about 1330 for a half hour ride to the Sanctuary. As we approached the entrance there was a Bald Eagle waiting for us in a tree along the river. We had a 90-minute guided tour along levees that defines wetland and pond areas. This was followed by a visit to their museum with a mounted bird collection and a stop at their gift shop and bookstore. Lots of geese. Blue-wing Teal. Northern Shovelers. Several Western Sandpiper, Lesser Yellow-legs, and

Willets. Several Redwing Blackbirds. A few Great Blue Herons. The bellow of Bullfrogs and the chirp of tree frogs. Turtles sunning on a log. Purple Loosestrife. Goldenrod. Invasive Himalayan Blackberries with pale pink flowers. Holly. Pearly Everlasting.

The busses returned us to the hotel about 1630. About 1800 we began our 15-minute walk through the park to the BBQ site. Beer. Chicken. Salmon. Beer. Potato salad. Beer. Ron Merritt and Gene LeBoeuf played guitars and sang. I presented my BASH play with audience participation. Interesting what beer and spontaneous reactions can produce.

August 17th

Wednesday I played hooky for the morning session and went down town with Carol.

Richmond had really changed in six years. It had been out in the country beyond the bus line and was largely into truck crops such as potatoes, onions and cabbage. It still produced a lot of vegetables and had several wineries but had urbanized. It was now the largest oriental community in Canada and the third largest Chinatown in North America after San Francisco and New York.

Vancouver was the largest metropolitan area in western Canada. City planners exported their Vancouver model where they plan complete high-density communities within the city. Each was complete with all the necessities such as food, entertainment, education, housing and business spaces. Areas were Downtown with museums and parks including Stanley Park), Gastown (gentrified old buildings along the river), Chinatown (oldest in Canada, Dr. Sun-Yat-sen home and classical Ming garden that I visited last trip), Westend (includes the gay community), Yaletown (up-scale), South Granville, Richmond (the island that became a city), and North Shore with Grouse Mountain Park and the Capilano Suspension Bridge. With excellent transportation, leisure and sporting facilities this was slated to be the home of the 2010 winter Olympic Games. We did not have time to see much.

An articulated 80 passenger bus took us for a 45 minute ride to Harbour Centre for $3.25. We passed numerous spas and gyms and signs in Chinese, Vietnamese and Punjabi.

Real estate was high. A 1500 sf in Richmond ran about $400K. In Downtown the same house would be a million bucks plus.

Anything Store

We walked past the harbor and into Gastown with its old steam powered clock. Flower baskets hung from the lampposts. Up one side of the street and back on the other. Hills aboriginal art was the only one I remembered from last trip. We had Italian for lunch at a sidewalk restaurant.

Gastown Steam Clock

Toot! Toot! Toot! Toot!
The steam clock tooted the quarter
This 19th century wonder
Is almost buried in the hanging flowers.

* * *

We stopped to see Storyeum. This was a relatively new living history production covering a square block in underground Vancouver. Well done.

After lunch we walked to Yaletown for art galleries. About 5:30 we arrived at a restaurant called "C" on the waterfront. Good food, outstanding service, and a really high bill.

We were back at the hotel by 9PM.

August 18th

The Grayline shuttle picked us up at 0830 for a ferry ride to Victoria. The bus drove on board and we got off to enjoy the ride. The driver said that most of the retired weathermen in Canada retired to Victoria since the weather is the same every day. Over half the population of Vancouver Island (700,000) lived around Victoria.

The weather was clear and mild and the tide was out exposing pink starfish on the pilings. During the trip I saw other ferries, seaplanes, container ships, sailboats of different sizes, several kinds of fishing boats, and a Canadian Coast Guard cutter but no whales, eagles, or seals.

We reboarded the bus, debarked, and began a half-hour drive to Butchart Gardens. The Garden had been a quarry for the Buchart concrete works that provided concrete for the developing Victoria in the late 1800s. When the limestone quarry was mined out in about 1900 Mrs. Butchart decided the old quarry would make a fine garden. She imported plants from around the world and personally oversaw the development and planting of the various gardens. A few of her friends began visiting to admire her handiwork. After a few years the visitors numbered in the thousands and an admission was charged. The garden is still privately owned. Admission was $11 US. The garden had landscape lighting for summer evenings and fireworks displays on Saturday nights.

We had an hour and a half—not nearly enough. The walk began passing the visitor center and coffee shop and through Waterwheel Square. There was a display of cyclamens and fushias. A half-mile trail lead around and through the former quarry with ponds, hills, a fountain and numerous trees and flower beds. Next was a concert lawn and stage, a pair of large totem poles, the Sturgeon fountain and the rose garden. We wandered through the Japanese Garden, passed the Star Pond and entered the Italian Garden. There were two restaurants, an ice cream shop, a display greenhouse, a plant identification office, and a Mediterranean garden. It was all handicapped accessible. I shot about 80 pictures.

Most memorable were beds of begonias of mixed colors and the rose beds planted with contrasting tall blue larkspur. I was a little disappointed in the selection of books in the book store. Their ice cream was made on site and delicious.

Butchart Gardens

"What can we do with a borrow pit
After the limestone has been mined out"
Asked Mr. Butchart.
"Well", says his wife.
"I think I will plant a garden"
She found the plants.
She scaled the walls.
She moved the rocks.
She planted her garden
And her dream came true.

*　　*　　*

The bus pulled through an exclusive high-end subdivision with multimillion-dollar 5,000-10,000 sf homes along the bay. Francis Rattenbury, who won the design competition for the legislative buildings and the Empress Hotel, designed and built many of them.

After seeing Mile Zero on the Trans Canada Highway the bus dropped everyone off at the various hotels. We had reservations at the Laurel Point Inn and arrived about 1800. After checking in we walked towards downtown for supper.

A couple of blocks along a pedicab stopped and offered a quick tour of town and several good restaurant recommendations. We took the tour passing the government buildings and the museum and Thunderbird Park then up Government St. with its candy shops, galleries and the worlds only McDonalds with a two-story crystal chandelier. We passed the Bastion Square (site of old Fort Victoria), Market Square (the heart of Old Town), and Bay Center (used to be the Hudson's Bay Company), the Christmas store and city hall.

We finally arrived at the gate to Chinatown, the Gate of Harmonious Interest, and Fan Tan Alley. Here even the dragon shaped street lights are privately owned. He showed us the Chinese school, little alleys where gambling and opium dens were once located and explained the half addresses where a hidden floor was built between the window top of the first floor and the second floor to avoid taxes.

He next peddled back along Wharf St. and recommended several restaurants with harbor views. We ate at thc Bravo. I had elk and Carol had steak but both were tough and chewy and the service was less than I expected considering the price. Or, maybe, because of the price.

Victoria Views

Sea planes.
Water taxis.
The Empress Hotel.
Pedicabs.
Clear blue skies.

* * *

We walked back to the hotel along Wharf St. to Government St. passing the Empress Hotel. The Empress was built on an old swamp that had been filled with refuse and rubble. It has settled several feet over the past hundred years and still sinking.

The Empress Hotel

Built on a swamp
It continues to sink
The Empress Hotel
It's not what you think.

A giant hotel
Covered with vines
Formal High Tea is still served
Just like in old times.

Its sits there alone
Looking over the bay
Hoping you will return
To Victoria someday.

* * *

We turned at Belleville St along the harbor where carvers, jugglers, and singers entertained the tourists. We were back at street level near the wax museum and the ferry docks. The full moon was just rising over the harbor.

Victoria had numerous parks and historical sites but we were leaving next morning. It also had diving tours, an underwater garden display and whale watching tours.

August 19th

I was up at sunrise and went for a walk. The tide was out but the rock were not accessible being 7-10 feet below the headwall. The mud was silty and the rocks were covered with green algae (<u>Enteromorpha</u> <u>sp</u>. and <u>Ulva</u> <u>sp</u>.) Beach Isopods (<u>Alloniscus</u> <u>perconvexus</u>) and Speckled Pillbugs (<u>Cirolana</u> <u>harfordi</u>) plowed through the seaweed and debris. Spot-bellied Rock Crabs (<u>Cancer</u> <u>antennarius</u> and Porcelain Crabs (<u>Petrolisthes</u> <u>cinctipes</u>) glided smoothly over the rocks covered by a couple inches of clear water. Carapaces of Shield-backed Kelp Crabs (<u>Pugettia</u> <u>producta</u>) and strands of Giant Kelp (<u>Macrocystis</u> <u>pyrifera</u>) lay amidst the rocks. There were broken shells of California Mussels (*Mytilus californicus*), Chubby Mya (*Platyodon candellatus*), Giant Pacific Oyster (*Crassostrea gigas*) and Pacific Oysters (*Ostrea lurida*). Acorn Barnacles (*Balanus glandula*) and Little Brown Barnacles (*Cthamalus dalli*) and several species if limpets encrusted the rocks.

Bright and early this Friday morning we were checked out and waiting for the tour bus at 0815. After a couple more passenger stops we were on our way to Port Hardy 500km north.

On the way to the village of Duncan we passed over the top of a 1000-foot ridge called Mount Todd. It had been a barrier to getting to Victoria and the southern part of the island from the northern part of the island. A highway was constructed in the 1920s and is part of the Trans Canada Highway leading the official ferry crossing at Nanaimo.

The first leg of the trip was to Duncan in the Cowichan Valley. The valley is famous for its agricultural products. The town is a bedroom community for Victoria and home to about 2500 of the First Nation Cowichan Band. There was a Native Heritage Center with historical displays and craftsmen demonstrations of carving and weaving. They advertised excellent fishing in the Cowichan and Koksilah Rivers and tours of several of the local wineries. The poet, Robert Service, once lived in the area. We got a windshield tour of town and saw many of the 85 totem poles that grace the town. The preferred term is story poles since they tell a story and are not worshipped. This town has no chain eateries.

Story Poles

Along the roadside were a number of intrusive Scotch Broom plants without leaves or blooms. This plant was first introduced about 1850. It has been highly invasive all over the Northwest.

It was easy to identify the First Nation reserves. They were not subject to Provincial restrictions and had fast food outlets, bill boards and cigarette shops.

Columbia Forest Museum Park was north of Duncan. This 100 acre park had a 1.5 mile narrow gage railroad that took visitors on a tour of a 19th century lumber operation.

The next stop was Chemainus. This village (pop. 400) had been about to die when the sawmill closed in the 1982. The citizens came up with a plan to paint murals on some of the buildings. This drew visitors. Galleries and other tourist trade shops opened. More murals were commissioned and there were currently 35 murals plus large wooden carvings. Population had increased to about 5000. They began presenting plays and had built a new theatre. The lumber business had also returned.

Mural

Another few minutes north we bypassed a 140-foot bungee jump into the Nanaimo River gorge. We also bypassed Nanaimo, Vancouver Islands second largest city and major ferry port. It was an important 19th century coal mining area. Off the coast lies Newcastle Island that was the source of coal for the Canadian-Pacific Steamship Company. The island is now one of the many Provincial Marine Parks. There were numerous trailer parks and golf courses. Nanaimo had a shipyard and was the official ferry continuation of the Trans Canada Highway from Victoria to Vancouver. The highway number highway north changed from Canada 1 to Canada 19.

We saw a lot of logs floating at Nanaimo but there was not much new timber cutting along the highway. The cut areas were mostly clear cuts. There were a few cuts where seed tree stands had been left. The most areas had not been burned or replanted. No ferns. No young trees. Piles of slash. Maples, alder, and aspen growth were getting thick. There were several planted areas where young pines were maybe 8-10 years old. Some areas had been planted in hemlock since it grew faster and brought a better price. Apparently there were few natural wildfires since there was not much lightning.

A few minutes later we turned off the highway into Qualicum vollage to drop a family off at the railroad station. This was the end of the passenger line. This was a nice looking retirement town with fishing and golf. Qualicum Beach was several miles from downtown and was several miles of granite sand. Lots of picnickers and clam diggers.

Granite Sand Beach

We stopped at a rest stop. I was surprised to see an Artic Lupine, and a lilac bush in bloom in August.

A six-foot deer fence was installed along the highway. This was supposed to keep deer and elk off the highway.

Lunch was at the Old Country Market at Coombs. This was unique in that the roof was sodded and goats were grazing on the roof. We had lunch and bought some fresh cherries and black berries. There were several tourist shops, an antique shop, and a wild-west trading post. Kids were kept occupied by an old VW hulk and a play castle.

Coombs Store

Mid afternoon break was at the Cable House restaurant in the Comox valley. The building was been built by a Mr. Duncan. He wrapped 8000 feet of old 2-inch lumber cable around a metal frame.

Nurse tree

There were a number of ancient rusting vehicles of various kinds, metal sculptures, and several outhouse style buildings with scenes painted on them. Good fresh pie and hot chocolate. There was also a gift shop. A large downed tree trunk called a nurse tree was all punky lay and covered with seedling conifers.

Cable House

We passed through Cortney and bypassed the RCAF base at Comox and the turnoff to the Mount Washington Ski Resort.

It began to drizzle and about half hour from Port Hardy we saw a couple black bears. The Quarterdeck Motel was away from down town and had its own marina and restaurant. A couple of years ago a black bear had brought a salmon for lunch into the hotel and plopped down on the rug in the lobby. They ran it off several times and finally had to shoot it as a dangerous pest. They said they had to clean the rug several times to get the odor out.

I took a walk in the drizzle along the beach at low tide. The rocks were slippery with algae (*Enteromorpha* sp). There were a few broken shells but nothing fresh. Little Brown Barnacle (*Cthamalus dalli*). California Shield Limpet *(Collisella pelta)*. Common Blue Mussel (*Mytilus edulis*). Fine-ribbed Cardita *(Cyclocardia cribricostata)*. Common Washington Clam (*Saxidomus nuttalli).* Bentnose Macoma (*Macoma nastua*). Smooth Pacific Venus *(Chione fluctifraga)*. Frilled California Venus (*Chione undatella*). Some of the shells were broken and could have come from the restaurant. Some may not be native.

August 20th

It was still misty at sunup. We packed up, checked out and waited for the shuttle to the ferry.

The ferry at Bear Harbor was pulled up with the bow open. We walked on with a number of other passengers. Some passengers were going to Prince Rupert or Queen Charlotte Island while others were going catch the train to Calgary. There were a few cars and trucks for passengers who would drive to Calgary.

We found our stateroom—two bunks and a shower and adequate storage. Main problem was it was on deck seven with no elevator to that deck.

I went topside to watch the departure. Land disappeared quickly into the mist as we entered Queen Charlotte Strait. Pacific White-sided Dolphin (*Lagenorhynchus obliquidens)* escorted us out.

Inland Passage

Several small islands drifted by as dark shadows as we crossed about a hundred miles of open water across Queen Charlotte Sound. This was open to the Pacific. We finally ducked behind Calvert Island and into Fitz Hugh Sound and the Inland Passage.

We passed several houses and little white structures that were navigation signal lights. We passed a small community of Namu then passed between King and Hunter Islands. Further north were an abandoned Hudson's Bay trading post and a community called Bella Bella.

Namu Village

There was an abandoned sawmill at Swanson Bay. A few pilings and a tall red brick smokestack was still standing.

Next came an abandoned salmon cannery at Middale on Princess Island.

Several types of fishing boats cruised the waterway. Trawlers. Seiners. Crabbers with piles of traps. There were also tugs with one or more barges.

Swansons Bay

Lighthouse

Pink salmon were jumping and a black bear was spotted. Many waterfalls cascaded in several stages onto the beach.

Waterfalls

We went to supper as the sun was disappearing in the overcast. It was a nice buffet with BBQ, lamb and roast beef with Yorkshire pudding. I tried one of the local beers but it had too much hops for my taste. We talked with a veterinarian and his wife from Australia and the waitress from Newfoundland.

About 2100 we passed a coal and wheat loading port and the proposed site for a new container port connecting to the railroad to service primarily Chinese ships. We docked at Prince Rupert at 2230 stern first.

Prince Rupert sits at the mouth of the Skeena River on mainland British Columbia. It is 450 miles by road or rail to Prince George and then another 500 miles to Calgary. This was supposed to be one of the best deep water port sites in North America. There was a ferry to Queen Charlotte Island the home of the First Nation Haida Band.

I don't know what downtown looked like. The dock was south of town and it was the middle of the night.

We lowered the top bunk and crashed. The mattresses were about 18 inches wide and about an inch thick.

August 21st

I was up about 0500 and went down to the car deck to talk to the guy on watch. When he was relieved and I went ashore with him. He had been in the area over 30 years. His wife and kids had left and gone to the States. He said he had worked on the renovation of this ferry. It had been a Swedish party boat with a big hot tub on the car deck and sixteen bars scattered across the ship. Now he works on it. He also fished and cut wood. He said they had expected a couple million in the salmon run but only about ten percent had arrived. Those were mostly the pink salmon that we had seen.

He said there was a big museum in Prince Rupert, the Museum of Northern British Columbia, in half of a working cannery. There were also a couple nice sand beaches.

I walked along the parking lot and railroad track to the harbor full of fishing boats. There was a lot of grass, alder scrub, dandelion, and oxeye daisy (*Leucanthemum vulgare*). I took several pictures of Prince Rupert strung along the shore. Weather was about 14°C and about 100% humidity.

The tide was out and the beach steep and rocky. About 0630 they began loading passengers. A Belted Kingfisher (*Megaceryle alcyon*) went airborne from under the dock.

The ship left on time in the early sun. It was relatively clear and got better during the day.

Inland Passage

The islands and their trees were now visible. There were large quartz outcroppings and numerous waterfalls. Sun and clouds played over the trees. The dark spruce and lighter green pine and large areas of hemlock covered the islands. There were low fog banks and clouds were rising from spots in the woods

We talked with a young aboriginal who worked as a logger cutting trees. He was going to Vancouver Island to cut big trees for $450 a day. He said it was more dangerous and five men had been killed this year already. His baggage included several large chain saws.

There was also an aboriginal teenager who talked about computer games, skate boards, hunting and mischief just like a teenagers elsewhere.

In mid afternoon a humpback whale was spotted. I got several pictures. Another had been spotted earlier and an Orca had been spotted the day before that I had not seen. Isolated gulls and occasional terns passed by. Some of the logs floating in the waterway were resting places for several gull or terns.

We had burgers for lunch and I requested a tour of the bridge and engine room. The bridge was modern with radar and GPS. The engine room was all diesel with variable pitch props. There was an environmental unit (wastewater) with holding tanks and treatment before discharging overboard.

We met a cruise ship heading north, the Norwegian Cruise Line *Norwegian Spirit.*

Norwegian Spirit

We hit the buffet for supper. Salmon with dill sauce. Lamb and rice. Prime rib.

The sun set and we were to dock about 2200. The shuttle bus was waiting and dropped us off at the same motel we stayed in on the way up.

We were picked up the next morning and began the trip back to Victoria. The same stops were made in reverse order and we arrived in Victoria about sunset. The driver said a 1500 sf home in Port Hardy would run about $70,000. In Duncan it would run $200,000 and in Victoria it would run $400,000.

A taxi took us from the hotel to Chinatown and dinner at the Don Mee, a big chrome upstairs restaurant with everyone dressed in tuxes (Taiwan modern). I had squid and a Tsing Tao beer. Good food. We walked back and got to the harbor in time to see the lights on the capitol building.

Victoria Legislative Building

Built of brown granite and almost ugly
Well proportioned with
A copper dome and gold statue
A fairy tale of lights at night.

* * *

August 22nd

We were up and had breakfast in time to leave about 0900. Carol was going shopping while I went to the Royal British Columbia Museum archives. We would meet at 1200 for lunch.

The archives in Calgary had told me the mining claims registered in 1898 in the gold rush were stored in Victoria. The Victoria archives said, "What?". If they were there we could not find them. I also looked for any information on Mrs. Brown and her baby born at Fort McPherson on Christmas 1898. Again, no luck but there was a death certificate for a Sara Brown about the right age.

I asked about my aboriginal masks and was told to see the curator in charge. She told me there were several grades—tourist, museum, collector, and ceremonial. Mine were tourist grade.

Lunch was in the Sticky Wicket. Carol had a Sczeshuan burger and I had an oyster sandwich and a LaBatt Blue. Fortified, we walked several miles looking at antiques and galleries and returned to the hotel in mid afternoon. I dozed out in the hotel's Japanese garden watching the seaplanes and other harbor traffic.

Japanese Garden at the Laurel Point Inn in Victoria

Quarter acre pond
Surrounded by cherry trees
Irises and Japanese
Red maples, topiary
Black Pines, traditional
Islands in still water.

* * *

August 23rd

Next morning we were to catch the ferry to Seattle at 1030. I took a short walk to look at the house boats moored a couple blocks away.

We took a cab to the ferry landing instead of hauling everything several blocks. Customs took a couple minutes and we boarded the ferry for a two hour ride.

The ride was unexciting except for passing a large container ship. We debarked and picked up the bags. A few minutes in line and we were through US immigration and customs. We caught a taxi to the hotel then went out to look at several galleries and antique shops.

We had supper at McCormick's Fish House. I had a selection of oysters from several bays and Sacramento River sturgeon. Carol had steak.

August 24th

We caught a limo out to SeaTac airport for an 1100 Southwest flight. We were home about 2100. Good trip.

INVERTS

Alloniscus perconvexus Beach Isopods   Vic/PH

Cirolana harfordi Speckled Pillbugs	Vic/PH
Cancer antennarius Spot-bellied Rock Crabs	Vic
Petrolisthes cinctipes Porcelain Crabs	Vic
Pugettia producta Shield-backed Kelp Crabs	Vic
Mytilus californicus California Mussels	Vic
Mytilus edulis Common Blue Mussel	PH
Crassostrea gigas Giant Pacific Oyster	Vic
Ostrea lurida Pacific Oysters	Vic
Cyclocardia cribricostata Fine-ribbed Cardita	PH
Saxidomus nuttalli Common Washington Clam	PH
Macoma nastua Bentnose Macoma	PH
Chione fluctifraga Smooth Pacific Venus	PH
Chione undatella Frilled California Venus	PH
Balanus glandula Acorn Barnacles	Vic/PH
Cthamalus dalli Little Brown Barnacle	Vic/PH
Mytilus californicus California Mussels	Vic
Collisella pelta California Shield Limpet	PH
several species of limpets	
Strongylocentrotus purpuratus Purple Sea Urchin	
Pisaster giganteus Southern 2-color starfish	
Banana Slug	

BIRDS

Alcidinidae—Kingfishers

Megaceryle alcyon Belted Kingfisher	Prince Rupert

Anatidae—Ducks

Anas americana American Wigeon	Reifel
Anas clypeata Northern Shoveler	Reifel
Anas disors Blue-winged Teal	Reifel
Branta Canadensis Canadian Goose	all

Ardeidae—Herons
Ardea herodias Great Blue Heron   all

Buteoninae—Eagles
Haliaetus leucocephalus Bald Eagle   Reifel

Cathartidae—Vultures
***Cathartes aura* Turkey Vulture Vancouver Is**

Corvidae—Jays and Crows
Corvus caurinus Northwestern Crow   all

Fringillidae—Sparrows
Passerculus sandwichensis Savannah Sparrow Vancouver
Gaviidae—Loons
Gavia immer Common Loon   Reifel

Icteridae—Orioles
Agelaius phoeniceus Red-winged Blackbird   Reifel
Sternella neglecta Western Meadowlarks Vancouver

Laridae—Gulls and Terns
Sterna hirundo Commom Tern   all
Larus argentatus Herring Gull   all
Larus hyperboreus Gluacous Gull   all

Ploceidae—Weaver Finches
Passer domesticus House Sparrow   all

Scolopacidae—Sandpipers
Calidris mauri Western Sandpiper   Reifel
Catoptrophorus semipalmatus Willet   Reifel
Tringa flavipes Lesser Yellowlegs   Reifel

Sturnidae—Starlings

Sturnis vulgaris Starling   Vancouver

OTHER VERTEBRATES

Whales

Megaptera novaengliae Humpback Whale
Lagenorhynchus obliquidens Pacific White-sided Dolphin
Grampus orca Orca or Killer Whale

Mammals

Ursa major Black Bear

Herps

Rana catesbiancha Bullfrog
Hyla regilla Pacific Tree frog

PLANTS

These are plants seen that I could identify.

GREEN ALGAE

Enteromorpha *sp*. Sea lettuce
Ulva sp.

BROWN ALGAE

Macrocystis pyrifera Giant Kelp

RED ALGAE

Porphyra sp. Nori or Laver

FERNS

Althyrium filix-femina Lady Fern

GYMNOSPERMS

CUPRESSACEAE Cypress Family
Thuja plicata western redcedar

PINACEAE Pine Family
Abies ambilis amabilis fir
Picea marina black spruce
Picea sitchensis Sitka spruce
Pinus contorta var *contorta* shore pine
Pseudotsuga menziesii Douglas fir
Tsuga heterophylla western hemlock

DICOTYLEDONS

ACERACEAE Maple Family
Acer macrophyllum big leaf maple

APIACEAE Carrot Family
Heracleum maximum cow parsnip
Osmorhiza berteroi sweet-cicely

AQUIFOLIACEAE Holly Family
Ilex aquifolium English holly

ASTERACEAE Aster Family
Anaphalis margaritacea pearly everlasting
Cichorium intybus chicory
Cirsium arvense Canada thistle
Erigeron sp fleabane
Grindelia integrifolia entire-leaved gumweed
Hieracium gracile slender hawkweed
Lactucus muralis wall lettuce
Leucanthemum vulgare oxeye daisy
Petasites frigida coltsfoot
***Solidago Canadensis* Canada goldenrod**
***Sonchus asper* prickly sow-thistle**

BETULACEAE Birch Family
Alnus rubra red alder

Betula papyrifera paper or white birch

BRASSICACEAE Mustard Family
Lepidium virginicum **tall pepper grass**

CAPRIFOLIACEAE Honeysuckle Family
Symphoricarpos albus **snowberry**

CARYOPHYLLACEAE Pink Family
Stellaria media chickweed

ERICACEAE Heath Family

Arbutus menzeii Pacific Madrone, Arbutus

FABACEAE Pea Family
Lupinus articus **arctic lupine**
Melilotus alba **white sweet clover**
Robinia pseudoacacia **golden leaf false acacia**
Trifolium repens **white clover**

FAGACEAE Beech Family
Quercus garryana Garry Oak

GERANIACEAE Geranium Family
Geramium bicknellii Bicknell's cranesbill

ONAGRACEAE Evening-Primrose Family
Epilobium angustifloium fireweed

PAPAVERACEAE Poppy Family
Eschscholziz californica **California poppy**

PLANTAGINACEAE Plantain Family
Plantago lanceolata **ribwort plantain**
Plantago major **common plantain**

POLYGONACEAE Buckwheat Family

Rumex crispus curly dock

RANUNCULACEAE Buttercup Family
Ranunculus repens creeping buttercup

ROSACEAE Rose Family
Comarum (Potentilla) *palustris* marsh cinquefoil
***Malus fusca* Pacific crabapple**
***Rubus discolor* Himalayan blackberry**
***Sorbus sitchensis* Sitka mountain ash**

SALICACEAE Willow Family
***Populus balsamifera* ssp *tricocarpa* black cottonwood**
***Populus tremuloides* trembling aspen**

TYPHACEAE Cattail Family
Typha latifolia Cattail

INVASIVE SPECIES
Cytisus scoparius scotch broom
Lythrum salicaria purple loosestrife

Niagara Falls and Toronto

24 Aug-3 Sep 2009

Contents

Niagara Falls and Toronto
24 Aug-3 Sep 2009

My wife was looking for a short vacation. One of her friends suggested Niagara Falls staying at Niagara-on-the-Lake and then a few days in Toronto. I had driven through Buffalo NY in 1962 but had not seen Niagara Falls and had been to Montreal but not Toronto so why not.

For a bit of background. The Great Lakes and Niagara Falls began with glacial activity several million years back as a tropical sea with coral probably when the tectonic plate was south of the equator. Successive cycles of wet and dry deposited thick layers of salt beneath Lakes Huron and Michigan and parts of Lake Superior. This area became an inland lake archeologist call Lake Iroquois. Over several million years in this big depression a thick layer of limestone was deposited on top of the salt which was then covered with a highly resistant layer of dolomitic limestone. 100,000 years ago a mile thick ice sheet gouged out the individual lakes. About 12,500 years back the ice began to retreat and the melt water filled the lakes. The water level increased as the ice sheet melted and soon the lakes were connected drowning out some of the lowlands between the individual lakes. Lake Eire finally filled and began discharging water through the Niagara River over and escarpment that has become Niagara Falls. The Great Lakes water level has dropped and recovered several times during the past 8,000 years. Niagara Falls flow has been reduced to a trickle. Erosion during this time had moved Niagara Falls about six miles upstream. Current erosion rates range from less than an inch to as much as three feet a year so that in maybe 20,000 years

Niagara Falls will disappear, Lake Eire will drain and become a river, and the Great Lakes will become a sea level water course.

Currently the Great Lakes contain about 20% of the world's fresh water. Niagara Falls consists of three falls: American Falls between Prospect Point and Luna Island; Bridal Veil Falls (the smallest) between Luna Island and Goat Island; and Canadian/Horseshoe Falls between Goat Island and Table Rock.

In 2009, 28 million visitors were expected. Peak visitors has been 72,000 per day with approaching $3 billion spent per year.

Monday. Delta Airlines took off at 0710 for Atlanta. The flight was smooth over scattered clouds.

One of the passengers was a little unusual. He had a cat on a leash. He put on his back pack and put the cat on top of it. He rode without a pet carrier but the cat was very well behaved.

We arrived in Atlanta and took off a little late for Buffalo. The weather was clear.

The Appalachian Mountains run NE/SW and there were linier clouds that looked like con trails over the valleys. North of these mountains were a zillion small cotton ball clouds all the way to Buffalo.

We landed a little after lunch and picked up our rental car at Enterprise. Carol had made the reservation with Enterprise and I suggested she look at Expedia. She got the car for 30% less. Enterprise up graded us to a Tiburon. This was a nice two door without much trunk space. However, the back seat folded down. It ran well but I had a gripe about bumping my head getting into the car and difficulty finding the seat belt over my shoulder.

We had instructions on getting to Niagara Fall but we got lost several times and drove 140 miles to cover the 20 to the bridge. We set the GPS for our destination in Canada but it refused to find anything north of the border so we had turned it off. Once across the border we saw signs for our destination—Niagara-on-the-Lake. Coming back to the US we cheated the system and turned the GPS on as we crossed the bridge. We had no trouble finding the Buffalo airport.

We drove through Niagara Fall, Ontario, and had our first view of the falls. Impressive. Road signs lead us towards Niagara-on-the-Lake and I stopped at the first fruit stand to ask directions to the particular address. An old French lady said she did not know and waved us on along the road.

After wandering around town and crossing the same streets several times I finally found a man with a map who pointed out the location. Our bed and breakfast was in the NW corner of town near the entrance to the Welland Canal. Lots of history in this area.

The B&B was an old house with three bedrooms for rent. It would become an inn if there were more than three. The gardens needed tending but our room was comfortable and the food was good. The B&B was run by a couple from Ireland. The breakfasts were large and good.

Our bed and breakfast was in the NW corner of town near the entrance to the Welland Canal. Lots of history in this area. The first canal was opened in 1829 partially to divert water to a grist mill near Port Colborne on Lake Erie. Later modifications straightened and deepened the canal and moved the first lock to St. Catharine on Lake Ontario. There are eight locks that change water level 326.5 ft. The canal is 26 miles and takes an average of 11 hours for passage. Shortly after the canal was opened lampreys enter Lake Erie. Numerous other exotic organisms have passed through the locks invading the Great Lakes.

Tuesday. Carol had made reservation for a tour on the computer. The tour included double-decker bus transportation, the Journey Behind the Falls at Table Rock Visitors Center, a tram ride over Whirlpool Rapids, and the Maid of the Mist boat ride. We parked in a municipal lot a mile from the tour for $15 for the day. The Niagara Falls area has been the most tourist developed of any of the major parks.

The bus was an old English double-decked bus. The tour company had bought 20 of them for local tours. The bus made a run up river a couple of miles explaining the sights such as the Old Scow sunk above the Falls and tales about going over the Falls.

First time I rode a double-decker bus was in England. We had landed at Mildenhall RAFB and were riding into London. I had a seat topside in the front row. It was a strange sensation to go into a roundabout backwards since they drove on the left side of the road.

The bus turned around and stopped at Table Rock Center for the Journey Behind the Falls. Table Rock visitor center has had a $32 million renovation with parking, food and souvenirs with a 360° theatre called Niagara's Fury and Journey Behind the Falls. An elevator dropped 151 ft to 600 feet of tunnels and an outside balcony and two short tunnels that had viewing areas. The trip comes with a plastic poncho.

While waiting for the bus I watched people. I don't think I had ever seen such a crowd as the people walking along the river.

Table Rock Center was well landscaped considering the cool moist conditions. I saw a couple Herring Gulls (<u>Larus</u> <u>argentalus</u>) cruising over the parking lots, some Bronzed Grackles (<u>Quiscalus</u> <u>versicolor</u>) running under parked cars, and House Sparrows (<u>Passer</u> <u>domesticus</u>) in the shrubbery.

The next stop was at the Whirlpool Aero Car. The Niagara River canyon makes a near right angle turn resulting in a turbulent situation that produces large short-term whirlpools. There is no permanent whirlpool.

A 3600 foot cable car ride built in 1916 crosses the corner over the whirlpools and back. Very large and deep whirlpools occur that are spectacular. There was also a jet boat ride that came up river and into some of the whirlpools.

The bus proceeded down river passing the Niagara Parks Botanical Gardens, the longest golf course in Canada, the School of Horticulture with the Butterfly Conservatory, and a brief stop at the 40 foot floral clock. The clock's 2000+ plants are replanted twice a year.

The tour concluded at the foot of Clifton Hill. We walked to the place where the Maid of the Mists was loading. We walked down the switchbacks in the cliff side about 150 feet to the dock. The two ferry boats take about 200 people each for a fifteen minute ride past American Falls, Bridal Veil Falls, and near Horseshoe Falls. The ride was cold and wet so everyone was issued a plastic poncho. The ride provides some remarkable close up views of the three Falls. The ride has operated since 1846.

Back in downtown Niagara-on-the-Lake we stopped for supper and found our way home in the misty dusk.

Pickup trucks stripped of their doors and beds used to harvest fruit were heading home. Prime picking season had passed but there was still plenty of fruit to harvest.

There was no sunset as such. It just got darker.

Wednesday. It was misting so we went down town to see the six art galleries. One was a photo gallery. One was crafts. The other four were interesting local artists. Carol bought a giclée (computer print on canvas) and a fancy jacket in one of the boutiques. I bought an ice cream cone for $3.50.

After it stopped drizzling we went out to Fort George. This Revolutionary Era fort had been built in 1796 across the river from Fort Niagara. During the War of 1812 the fort was destroyed in May of 1813 and finally abandoned in 1820. The Fort has been restored to pre-1813 appearance and opened as the Fort George National Historic Site in 1950. The officer quarters were nice but the enlisted lived in much more

Spartan conditions. Enlisted families lived in a corner of the barracks separated by sheet walls.

We left in late afternoon to find our way to the 525 foot tall Skylon Tower for supper in their revolving restaurant. The view of the Falls from the tower was excellent. They had a special dinner menu for $30 that included the elevator ride. Their prime rib was pretty good.

After supper we looked at the two First Nation Seneca casinos. A white multistory modern sugary-style facility, the <u>Casino Niagara</u>, was situated alongside many of the area's hotels. It is. The other, <u>Niagara Fallsview Casino Resort</u>, was a multistory building that was part of big entertainment complex, the <u>Fallsview Tourist Area</u> that had been one of the biggest commercial construction projects in the Province.

Thursday. I was out in the backyard before breakfast. A female Ruby-throated Hummingbird (<u>Archilochus</u> <u>colubris</u>) was feeding and a pair of black poll warblers (<u>Dendroica</u> <u>striata</u>) was in the trees. A small flock of Canadian Geese (<u>Branta</u> <u>Canadensis</u>) was flying north towards the lake.

After breakfast we started out to see the botanical center. We stopped at an art museum along the way. It was the retirement home built by a famous local lawyer who had himself buried in the front yard. The museum had a big collection of early pioneer and Indian art, paintings of Niagara Falls, and early Canadian bronzes.

The Niagara Parks Botanical Gardens and School of Horticulture was about 30 acres including the gardens, landscaping school, student dormitories and the Butterfly Conservatory. There was no entry fee to the garden but the butterfly conservancy was $15 each. We toured the butterfly house. As we were leaving there was an announcement that a butterfly had escaped through the airlock into the gift shop. That is one of the dangers of displaying exotics—thy might get out and get established possibly messing up the local ecology.

We started on the garden walk when Carol spotted a horse drawn carriage ride that cruised through the park. The carriage driver gave us a guided tour of most of the park without the walking.

The horticulture school was a highly regarded training center for landscapers. They take 20 students a year for a three year course. Cost is about $5,000 for Canadians and $15,000 for foreigners including room. The students do the work in the gardens and each has a multiyear research project.

We left about 2PM to go to a winery for a tour. The winery was one of about 70 in the area. It had been in business for about 30 years. The winery covered over 200 acres. This winery grafted all its own vines on native root stock and was unusual since it did not buy or sell grape juice from anyone else. The vines were raised on wires rather than V posts or T posts. There were several windmills at $10,000 each to protect the vines against early cold snaps and a series of gas canons were used to keep the birds away. The rows were mulched with leas and plastic mulch and pesticides were not used. Rose bushes were used at the ends of the rows as an indicator of pests, nutrition and soil condition.

Next we went underground 30 feet to the pressing room. The grapes were crushed and trash was removed. Depending on the type of wine to be made the skins were removed immediately for white wine, left for a few days for blushes, or left in the juice for about three weeks for red wines to add appropriate color. The juice is then pressed and the juice held for several months for fermentation.

The wine is then bottled. The guide did not mention killing the yeast and sterilizing the wine to stop fermentation in the bottle.

I asked about sparkling wines. (Sparkling wines are not killed and have a little sugar added to continue a little fermentation for bubbles. Too much sugar makes too much gas that can break the bottles or cause most of the wine to escape on opening.) The guide was not clear on this.

We tasted several wines. Nothing great. The guide told about making ice wine where the grapes are allowed to freeze, picked at night in freezing weather and are crushed frozen before fermenting. The process is much more expensive in labor, equipment, and processing and makes an expensive sweet desert wine that was selling for $70 a quarter liter (about 8 oz). No sampling.

The winery was setting up for a wedding. I noticed one lady with and electric iron pressing the table cloths after they had been put on the tables.

We had supper at the Charles Inn. Food and service was good but the price was high.

Friday. We packed up and loaded the car to return to Buffalo airport to catch the bus to Toronto. Breakfast was full of discussion of Toronto and what to see. We were served potato scones and sausages and scrambled eggs with a spicy sauce that tasted much like A-1.

We got the driving instructions and entered the US across the Rainbow Bridge to avoid the heavy morning traffic. Once across the bridge and out of Indian Territory we set up the GPS that worked fine in the US. We were to the airport in less than an hour.

We turned in the car and caught the bus. We had to go into Buffalo to buy tickets. We left for the two-hour ride to Toronto about 1330.

It took almost an hour to go through customs in a really ratty immigration and customs office.

The roadside was green with grapes on the fences and stands of Queen Anne's Lace and Goldenrod. Wet spots were filled with Arundo and invasive Phragmites. Biodiversity at this time of the year was limited.

We passed one area along the lake where several kite surfers were doing their best to ride minimal waves. The sky was cloudy with a temperature of 18°C (65°F).

About an hour later we hit rush-hour traffic entering first Hamilton and then Toronto. We got off at Union Station about ten blocks from our hotel. A ten dollar cab ride took us the rest of the way.

After we unpacked we had supper in the hotel restaurant—their pre-theatre special.

The room was a suite with living room, bedroom, dressing room and a separate tub and shower. There were two large flat screen TVs and a small refrigerator.

Saturday. We left the hotel about ten and went to a big mall, the Eaton Center, for a little shopping and breakfast.

About noon we took the subway to visit Casa Loma. This was the home built by Sir Henry Mill Pellatt a prominent banker and military man. He hired architect E. J. Lennox to help him built his dream of a medieval castle overlooking Toronto. Construction began in 1911 and took three years costing $3,500,000. The Pellatts lived there about ten years before they went bankrupt. The city took over the castle and rented it to the Kiwanis Club who restored and operated the facility since 1937. The castle is furnished and has beautifully landscaped grounds.

Back at the Eaton Center we had supper at the Baton Rouge which was not a Cajun restaurant. I had lobster ravioli which was very good and a Guinness. Carol had a steak.

Sunday. We decided to get a ticket for the double-decker bus. The ticket was $30 each and good for a week. It was a sightseeing bus that you get on or off at their stops. It had two routes so we took one route complete and then took the other route to the Scotiabank Busker Fest for Epilepsy. This was about four blocks of vendors selling everything and singers, jugglers, and other entertainers. Interesting afternoon.

A bagpiper was playing on the corner where we waited for the bus. Interesting to watch but it sounded so good when he quit.

We stopped in an English pub for supper. I had Sheppard's Pie and an IPA. Carol had fish and chips. This was a town of pubs with one on practically every corner.

Monday. After breakfast we took the double-decker bus to the waterfront. The waterfront from Front St south was built over the old waterfront and railroad yards from fill dredged from the harbor. This area is covered with office buildings and condos.

According to advertising the harbor area was full of craft shops and art galleries. Truth is there were one gallery and an Inuit museum and a group of crafters making glass and metal works and a lot of million dollar condos overlooking the harbor. The galleries and the Inuit museum were closed since Monday is an international down day for galleries. The craft area consisted of several shops separated from visitors who were restricted to a glass-lined hallway where visitors could see crafts people at work.

We went on a harbor boat ride. The ride cruised the waterfront before crossing to the three islands—Ward's, Algonquin, and Centre. There are permanent residents but no cars on the islands. The local ferry from Toronto brings over a few commercial vehicles for their deliveries. We passed Hanley Point the first full-time family lived and made a stop on Centre Island that was developed as a park. We returned along the eastern waterfront to the dock.

Water fowl of the islands included, Canadian Geese (<u>Branta Canadensis</u>), Mute Swans (<u>Cygnus olor</u>), Anhinga (<u>Anhinga anhinga</u>), and the Eastern Belted Kingfisher (<u>Megaceryle alcyon alcyon</u>).

There was fountain with bronze salmon leaping up stream.

We headed back to the hotel. I noted large metal recycling containers near the corners that had separate slots for recyclable, paper and trash. In the airport in Buffalo there were compactor recycling containers for plastics and newspapers. Toronto also charges a nickel fee for plastic bags.

Tuesday. Today was museum day. We caught the subway to the Royal Ontario Museum near Queen's Park. The north side of the building along Bloor St was a modern façade the Michael Lee-Chin's Crystal building.

The first level was the museum store, learning center, lecture rooms and lunch room.

On lever 2 the natural history displays. The mineral collection was outstanding. There were birds, dinosaurs, mammals, a bat cave, marine life, and several discovery collections.

Level 3 was cultural collections with a good mix of areas and displays.

Level 4 contained costumes and textile exhibits and the Institute of Contemporary Culture.

Level 5 was a restaurant that was also open evenings.

We took the subway to the Art Gallery of Ontario. This is a modern museum of mostly Ontario art collections such as Thompson collections of ship models, Canadian art and photography and the Henry Moor sculpture collection. Carol decided not to see this.

We did go to the museum store. They had books, prints, statuary, and masks. The Indian artifacts were Inuit, Seneca, Algonquin but no western tribes. I checked their prices.

We headed for the CN tower for supper. The ride up the 1500 foot tower took about two minutes. The revolving restaurant took 72 minutes per revolution. The CN stands for the Canadian National Railroad that built the tower. The view was nice but not as interesting as from the tower in Niagara. To the southwest were the cities of Mississauga, Burlington, and Hamilton. To the east was Oshawa. The southern lake shore was visible on the horizon.

Supper was good and the service was as good as you could want. Taxi, supper and tip came to $140.

Wednesday. We took the bus to the CN tower to finish up our tour ticket. We did not get to the zoo or the Children's Museum since they were both outside of town to the east. We also did not get into the 70 miles of tunnels connecting the downtown area.

The tower elevator had a glass window so you can see the ground as the elevator does its thing. There was also a large glass plate in the floor so you could walk out over space. Many people refused to go near it.

We went to the Bata Shoe Museum housed in a museum shaped like a shoebox. I was surprised at the extent of the historical displays of shoes from around the world. The collection of North American Indian footwear was particularly interesting.

Back at the hotel we decided to go out for Thai for supper. Very good. I had a cup of lychee liquor for desert.

Thursday. We packed up and left for the bus station and were on our way to the airport about 1100. Customs took about an hour again through a ratty facility with major construction underway.

We were on our way and were home in San Antonio by10 PM.

After thoughts. The weather for this trip was enjoyable. 70's in the day time and 50's at night. Could hardly be better.

The city of Niagara was crowded and rather impersonal dealing with strangers. The falls were impressive.

Niagara-on-the-Lake was pretty and clean and felt more like visiting in-laws. Wine, apples, cherries, and history a plenty.

Toronto was a vanilla city. There were a lot of people working hard but the city struck me was not very exciting.

Enterprise North: Backdoor to the Yukon

Diary of Otto Lahser

Written During his trip to the Klondike
A Year's Journey (1898-1899)

edited by
Carl Lahser

Flat bottom York boat with passengers. The Enterprise was similar but had a steam engine and paddle wheel.

Enterprise North: Backdoor to the Yukon Diary of Otto Lahser

Written During his trip to the Klondike
A Year's Journey (1898-1899)

In 1898 my great uncle Otto Lahser and some friends in Detroit calling themselves "the Enterprise" set out for the gold fields of the Klondike. Besides my great uncle, Otto Lahser, members listed include J. Block, Mr. and Mrs. Braund, Sid Down, Ed Gautherat, Herman Groemer, Lew Miller, J. B. Wright. They decided to travel the "Backdoor Route" from the east through Canada rather than the western routes. Train, stage coach and freight wagon got them from Detroit, Michigan to Athabasca Landing, Alberta, where they built a steam powered wooden sternwheeler York boat called the "Enterprise". This craft transported them down the Athabasca River through Great Slave Lake and down the MacKenzie River. They sold the craft and portaged overland to La Pierre's House on the Bell River, then canoed down the Porcupine River to Fort Yukon where the diary entries stopto Athabasca Landing where they built a steam-powered York boat.

The location of the original hand written diary is unknown. Some of my earliest memories are of my father telling about his Uncle Otto's trip to the Klondike. A typed copy of this diary was given to me about 1980. The diary has been annotated for clarity and where it has been possible to confirm dates and incidents. Spelling and grammer are original. The following personnel and organizations have provided assistance: Mr. Richard Valpy at the Northwest Territories Prince of Wales Northern

Heritage Center in Yellowknife NWT; Ms Anne Morton, Archivist at the Hudson Bay Company Archives in Winnipeg, Manitoba; and Ms Eileen Hendy, Marilyn Mol and Robert Tannas of the Athabasca Archives in Athabasca, Alberta; Ms Lindsay Moir of the Glenbow Museum; Dr. Adreana Davies, director of the Alberta Museun Association; and Mrs Mary Weber-Blatz, administrator of the Fort McMurry Historical Society.

My great grandfather, Charles Adolph Lahser, was a wheelwright and wagon maker from the Schwaben area of southwestern Germany near Stuttgart and spoke Swabish. He had several children one of which was Otto who was born in 1877. Otto was raised near Cheboygan, Michigan, and moved with the family to near Detroit in the mid 1890s. Otto was reported to be about six foot five inches tall, and weighed about 250 pounds. He was powerful and liked to fight and gamble. Otto was 20 years old at the beginning of the diary. When Otto returned to Detroit he and his brother, Charles, bought and developed land around Round Lake and Clifford Lake near Brighton, Michigan. Otto, who retired at 35, was reported to have been involved in a gold mine deal in Columbia and land deals in Texas and Florida. He died in 1970 at the age of 93.

Tuesday, March 15, 1898

Left Detroit via CPR *(Canadian Pacific Railroad)* at 12:03 AM sun time in company with members of the Enterprise, M. H & Co. The depot was crowded to its utmost capacity with our friends, who gave us a hearty send off. Arrived at Toronto *(Ontario, Canada)* at 8 AM—nice town. Left about 1 o'clock PM. We were to get tourist sleeper at Carleton Junction. They have our dough, but sent car on ahead of us.

Wednesday, March 16th.

No tourist sleeper. At North Bay *(Ontario, Canada on Lake Nipissing 200 miles north of Toronto)* they attached a Colonization car and we secured two sections, but as our baggage is not on this train, we started out on the boats without blankets. Stove in car and we had hot tea and coffee.

Thursday, March 17th.

Cold. Went past the north shore of Lake Superior. About a foot of snow. No fire in car. Laid over at Rat Portage one hour; done some shopping; nice town.

Friday, March 18th.

Cold and clear; 8 below at Winnipeg. Arrived at Winnipeg *(Manitoba, Canada)* at 3 AM. Changed cars; laid over 1 1/2 hours; changed cars at Brandon *(Manitoba, Canada)*. We are going over the plains; can see twenty miles each way. Prairie chickens, rabbits and coyotes plentiful. Snow one to two feet deep. We passed through Manitoba Province and Assinobia. We can see plenty of antelope.

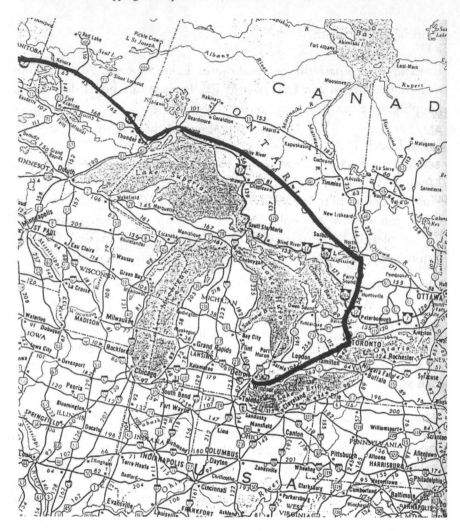

Map 1. Detroit Michigan to Winnipeg Manitoba

Saturday, March 19th.

Zero. We are wheeling through Assinobia (*south central Saskatchewan, Canada*), a rolling prairie; lots of fair sized herds of cattle on the prairie. We laid over at Medicine Hat (*southeastern Alberta, Canada*) for two hours. We meet with Indians in every town. We arrived at Calgary (*south central Alberta, Canada*) at 3 PM and secured quarters at the Royal Hotel. (*The Royal Hotel was located ear the train station and the Hudson's Bay Company near Stevens and Center Streets. Otto was listed as a guest in the*

Calgary Daily Herald on 21 March 1898) After the Enterprise had given their provision order to Hudson Bay Co. *(Hudson's Bay Company (HBC))* I consented to cast my lot with them. Took a stroll about town and then a much needed rest. Temperature 50 above.

Sunday, March 20th.

Stormy, 10 above. This climate is delightful. The town is in a valley and on the south bank of the Bow River. In the AM we took a walk north, crossed the river and climbed the bank, 300 feet high. Can see the foothills of the Rocky Mountains. This is a rolling prairie, stock raising country. In the evening we concluded to send four boys to Edmonton to view the situation and secure quarters.

Monday, March 21st.

11 below. E. Gautherat, J. Block, H. Goermer and myself went to Edmonton *(Alberta, Canada, about 200 miles north of Calgary)*, leaving L Goermer, L. Miller and J. Wright to pick out our outfit outside of provisions. I ordered our eats to last 15 months. We were particular to get only the very best that could be procured, bacon and salt pork, fat and heavy olive oil, hard wheat and pastry flour, plenty of dried fruits and assortment of staple foods which we figured would carry us through, with the addition of fish and game, picked up enroute and for which we were well prepared with gill nets, rifles and shotguns and plenty of ammunition.

(March 22-26.
   ON THE TRAIL TO EDMONTON)

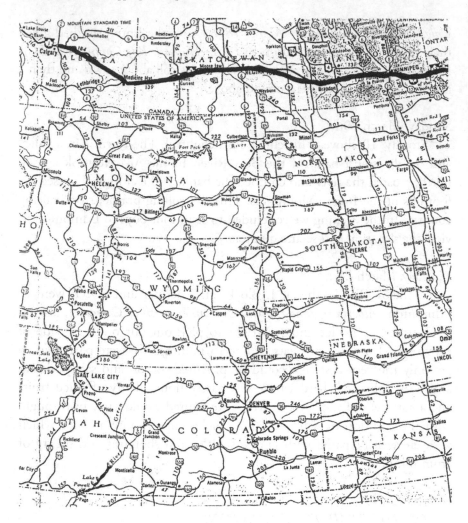

Map 2. Winnipeg, Manitoba to Calgary, Alberta

Sunday, March 27th.

30 below here in Edmonton. Edmonton proper is a couple miles north of South Edmonton, situated on the high banks of the Saskatchewan River. HBC fort is one mile down river. Visited Salvation Army at night. *(Both were on the north side of the river).*

Monday, March 28th.

A little below zero. I took L. Miller, H. Goermer, and J.B. Wright over to see Mr. Potter and they arranged for a course of lessons in placer mining (*possibly in the Strathcona area. Possibly an employee of the Walker Lumber Company that had mining interests and built boat for use on the Saskatchewan River. Placer mining was mining by washing, dredging, pumping or other hydraulic methods*). Our freight from Calgary arrived tonight.

Tuesday, March 29th.

Zero. I took out free miner's certificates for the N.W. Territories $10.00 and British Columbia $5.00. Made our final purchases of traps, mining tools, etc. Went over to Edmonton in afternoon. H. & L. Goermer and J.B. Wright left at 8 PM, bound for the landing 96 miles. (*Athabasca Landing now called Athabasca. HBC trading post on the Athabasca River*)

30 March to 2 April.

ON THE TRAIL TO ATHABASCA LANDING. (*Athabasca Landing Is about 90 miles north of Edmonton. There was a good HBC toll road for stage, wagon or sleigh. Freight cost $0.75 to $1.00 per 100 pounds. Another trail followed the Tawatinaw River.*)

Sunday, April 3rd.

I arrived at Athabasca Landing at noon; I broke away from the sleighs and walked the last 15 miles. Lew Miller, E. Gautherat and J. Block arrived at 2 P.M. An extra stage brought S. Down and Mr. and Mrs. Braund. This is all the gang. (*A Mrs. S. Brown is listed a Appendix IV of J. G. MacGregors' book, The Klondike Rush Through Edmonton, 1897-1898, as passing through Edmonton and making it all the way to the Yukon. Braund = Brown. Appendix III lists the Enterprise with 8 people passing through Edmonton. On page 168 there is a note that Mrs. Brown had a baby at Ft. MacPherson before making the crossing to La Pierre's House in March of '99. This was confirmed by Mrs. Craig as quoted in Melanie Mayer's Klondike Women. The "Enterprise" is also listed in the Edmonton Bulletin of 23 Aug. 1898 as leaving Athabasca Landing with 8 people and ten tons cargo.*)

Monday, April 4th.

30 to 50 above. We spent the day fixing up the camp. *(Camp was probably on the Tawatinaw River near the Athabasca since the water in the Athabasca would be silty.)* The population of this town consists of Klondikers. The only buildings are the Hudson Bay Co. post and a boarding house, also two saw mills. The town is situated on the south bank of the Athabasca River. *(According to MacGregor, Athabasca had two hotels, a restaurant, a butcher shop, half a dozen boat yards, four general stores, a barber shop, two bakeries and a Solomon Moses general store. This was apparently a couple months later.)*

Tuesday, April 5th.

Five of us went across the river and cut and lugged over enough wood to last us for our stay here; we also went to the saw mill 3 miles up river *(bigger trees grew several miles up river)* to get figures on lumber; price $31.50 per *(1000 board feet?)* feet delivered at landing. Braund got sick and we kept fire all night, she could not go to the boarding home. *(This may have been morning sickness resulting from her pregnancy.)*

Wednesday, April 6th.

30 above. We ordered our lumber from HBC and the most of it was sawed today. Braund still sick.

Thursday, April 7th.

We received the bulk of our lumber; went across the river and got four posts and planted them in the ground, on the shore next to the HBC's barn, to build our boat on.

Friday, April 8th.

35 above. We worked on the boat, got our keel and placed it face down on the posts.

Saturday, April 9th.

Warm. The snow is going fast, but they still haul on sleighs from Edmonton. We worked on the boat and built a dry kiln *(to dry the fresh cut lumber).*

April 10th, Easter Sunday.

Nice warm weather. Put in a quiet day in camp, that is, as quiet as the dogs would allow—some well matched dog teams here.

Monday, April 11th.

We put in a good day on the boat. Went across the river for sweeps, oars and pike poles; lumber is drying in good shape. We held a meeting at 8 P.M. and accepted the resignation of L. Goermer as captain. I was elected to fill vacancy. Braund out today.

Tuesday, April 12th.

Warm. Went across the river to cut timber and firewood. We got out Braund's punching bag and attracted a crowd of 25.

Wednesday, April 13th.

We got the use of Mr. Fraser's steam box (A *steam box was a portable steam generator used to bend wood for the boat*); also put on some of sides and bottom of boat and took a snapshot of her. After supper, we got out the bag and also had a tug of war, 75 men participating in sport. We had seven 1 1/2" x 8" x 30 ft. boards stolen last night.

Thursday, April 14th.

Warm. Burned 330 ft. boards last night. L. Goermer was in charge of it. Ice on river getting thin. A team smashed through last night. Hot game with bag.

Monday, May 2nd.

Warm. We have the boat ready for machinery, which we expect almost any day. Our 8 x 10 tent arrived today. Two loads, belonging to Lyster party, arrived today. We unloaded the same. (*The 4 Apr 98 Edmonton Bulletin reported that Dr. W.J. Lister, E.H. Sargent and C.A. Howell of Detroit owned the Michigan Northern Mining Company with capitol stock of $25,000. To explore the Peel*

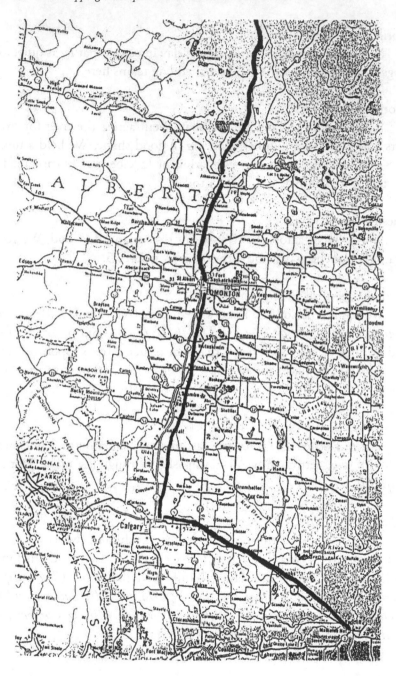

Map 3. Medicine Hat, Alberta through Calgary, Edmonton and Tthabasca Landing to near Ft McMurray, Alberta

River, they had a special screw-driven steel boat prefabricated in Detroit in 12 transverse sections for shipping and to allow portaging. It was 36 feet long with a two foot draught and weighed 2500 pounds and could carry 12 tons. It had a 16 hp engine. Dr Lister, with six others, was also reported bound for the Laird River in the Yukon Territory on the "Dr. Lyster" with 7 tons of cargo. The Laird was navigable to the lower end of Laird Canyon near Watson Lake and the Cassiar gold field.)

Tuesday, May 3rd.

Warm. Dr. Lyster, of Detroit, arrived at 10 A.M., having walked from foot of big hill. He ate dinner with us. Our boiler and engine arrived at 3 P.M. We had teamster drive to edge of boat and we put her in from wagon with skids and rope.

Wednesday, May 4th.

Clear. We worked on boat. Sid and Braund fitted up engine and boiler.

Thursday, May 5th.

Clear. No work on boat.

Friday, May 6th.

We put in the day fitting up boat.

Saturday, May 7th.

Clear; strong west wind. We fitted up boiler and engine and borrowed pipe enough from Dr. Lyster to connect them. In 30 minutes, with wood—not the best—we had 250 lbs. steam, The engine ran well and turned the big wheel. (*MacGregor states it was a sternwheeler. "Very strongly built and manned by some practical sailors from the Great Lakes. She sport a big staff and pennant." As reported in the* <u>Edmonton Bulletin</u>, *the "Enterprise" was a stern wheeler, 50 X 10 feet, drawing 18 inches.*) We decided to try her up stream tomorrow, if the wind is down.

Sunday, May 8th.

Heavy west wind. We are short some provisions, purchased at Calgary. We also want to make a few at Edmonton and want our mail looked up. It was proposed we send JBW to Edmonton by stage, which leaves here Tuesday AM. He and Sid Down consented to walk there and will start tomorrow AM. Will return by next Saturday PM. (*The snow was gone so the return trip was probably made on horse drawn wagon.*)

Monday, May 9th.

Clear. Sid Down and J.B. Wright left early this AM for Edmonton.

(No notes for 10-14 May.)

Sunday, May 15th.

Clear. We helped Dr. Lyster launch his steel boat. Will mention here that the water is lower at the present time than it was ever known to be, which will make it difficult for us and very dangerous.

Monday, May 16th.

Clear. We lined (*pulled up stream by lines*) our boat up to HBC warehouse and loaded our outfit. (*This indicates that their camp was on the Twottenow Creek to the east of town. HBC owned the land between the Twottenow and Mud Creeks.*) The stuff purchased at Edmonton by J.B. Wright, which should have been on stage Saturday PM, has yet not arrived. The stage has probably been discontinued. Dr. Lyster has consented to bring it on for us and we pull out tomorrow AM. In the evening, we went on the trip of Dr. Lyster's steel boat. They were trying the *Sparrow* at the same time, and we gave her the "go by." (*The "Sparrow" was a 60 foot propeller ship owned by George T. Leitch with 15 persons from Minneapolis with 7 tons of cargo. It was wrecked on Grand Rapids.*)

Tuesday, May 17th.

Clear. We had breakfast at 5 AM and pulled out of the landing at 5:50 AM. We stopped once for wood and before night we had passed seven rigs that had left on Sunday and Monday. We were hard on the bottom once; no damage. We stopped at 7:45 PM. Made 80 miles.

Wednesday, May 18th.

Clear. We steamed out at 6:30 AM. Arrived at Pelican Rapids (*about 120 miles down the Athabasca River*) about 2 PM. We tied up about one mile above and went down to investigate. We went down the right hand side of the bank within 15 feet of the bank. We got aground at foot of rapids; got off again and tied up for the night. J.B. Wright and I crossed over to the mouth of Pelican River and stoned a big mess of fish in the shallows.

Thursday, May 19th.

Cloudy. When we pulled out we came to more rapids, worse than Pelican. They were very numerous, rough and rocky, but we shot through them all. We went through the Dr. Jule Fow *(Joli fou)* rapids at AM. We saw boats in trouble all around us. We ran into more bad rapids between 11 and 12 o'clock. We were hung up on the rocks for three hours. We lightened about three tons and got in to our waists and made a channel. We broke one rudder and tied up for the night and put in a new one. Very exciting; made from 20 to 25 miles.

Friday, May 20th.

Clear. Pulled out at 7:30 AM and broke the new rudder going through first rapids. We ran about 8 miles, tied up at head of rapids and picked up our rudder but concluded to go on with only one. Going through the next rapids we struck several times, lost the other rudder and tied up about 8 miles above Grand Rapids at noon (*160 miles from Athabasca Landing*). Several parties are tied up here, among them the "Hamilton Boys" (*an 8 person party from Hamilton,*

Ontario, Canada), "The Sweeper Man Party" (*Not identifiable*). Miller, Down, and myself got into one of the dinkies and went down to Grand Rapids; they look desperate. It rained from 2 to 6 PM. We had lunch with four Winnipeg boys (*Three groups of four were listed for Winnipeg*) and returned on foot at 10:30 PM.

Saturday, May 21st.

Cool. We held a meeting with the members of the other outfits and concluded to help each other. We pulled out at 10 AM with one rudder and a sweep. Lost rudder #4 and tied up one mile above the island. We spent the afternoon sizing up the rapids. There is an island a half mile long in the center of the river. There is a drop of 67 ft. in 3/4 of a mile. The channel is on right hand side with hardly room to line a boat down between the boulders. The tramway on the island

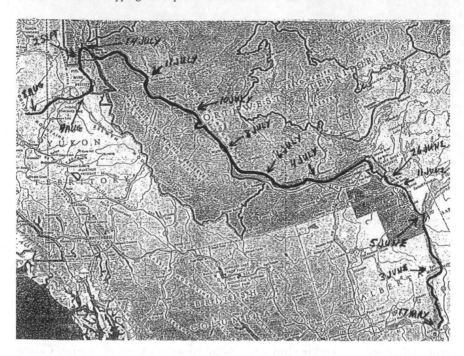

Map 4. Athabasca Landing, Alberta, down the Athabasca River to Great Slave Lake, down the McKensie River to Ft. McPherson and up the Peel River is owned by the Hudson Bay Co. The car is supposed to hold about one ton, $500 per load. The rapids appear to be nasty and can be heard for miles. Water raised 2 1/2 inches.

Sunday, May 22nd.

Clear. We tried to hire Captain Short *(Captain Short was also called Captain Shot, since he was the first to shoot the Grand Rapids. Also spelled Shott. Actual name was Louis Fousseneuve from Lac la Biech. He was born in St Boniface, Manitoba, in 1841 and died in Athabasca, 14 May 1914.)* to guide us to McMurry *(Fort McMurray)* and he said he would on his next trip. *(He charged $25 per trip but increased his charge to $100 per trip later in the season.)* Will return in 10 days. Water raised 4 inches. *(Water rose because of the thaw. High water was needed to get over many of the rapids and falls on the river. The Athabasca flows almost straight north for about 180 miles then turns east for about 80 miles to Ft McMurray. Then it flows north past Fort Mackay almost 200 miles to Lake Athabasca.)*

Monday, May 23rd.

Clear—cool. Ed, Jack and myself took one of the dinkies and went to the island. Saw Billy Smith, also Billy Connors (*Connors was a prominent trader from Edmonton who owned a trading post at Fort Smith*). We disconnected boiler and engine and put Enterprise in shape to handle her with oars and sweep. I went out hunting and found signs of moose and bear. At 11 PM we were attracted by a pair of eyes in the brush, but did not shoot as some of the boys were sleeping on the bank. Water raised 5 1/2 inches.

Wednesday, May 25th.

We were busy running up and down the river all morning. We hired the three stranded Frenchmen's boat to lighten ours and about 5:30 PM our guide and his crew came to take us over to the island. We were rigged with four oars and a sweep and we tied up at head of island without a hitch, but no go with the smaller boat, into which we loaded 3,000 lbs. A young Breed attempted to guide her over and he hit about every rock in the river. Before we got to the island, we had nearly the full load in small boats and most of us had a free bath thrown in, but we did not lose any of the outfit.

Thursday, May 26th.

Clear. We arose at 4 AM and packed 400 lbs. each before breakfast. Four of us poled the Frenchmen's boat over to the Police shack. By 4 PM we had complete outfit packed to the north end of the island, a distance of half mile. Old Captain Campbell gave us a treat. After supper, we went to look at our outfit and missed nearly all our bacon. We found them in Mr. Hendrick's boat, (*Possibly the Fargo parties' screw steamer, "Hendricks"*) tied up in small eddy; it was taken by mistake. The policemen took a photo of us while eating dinner. We got our big boat over just in time, as water lowered seven inches in last two days.

Friday, May 27th.

Clear. We arose as 4:15 AM and took the two dinkies over on the tram car. HBC men were sleeping. After eating, our guide and crew came to take our boat through rapids. The water was low, and we had a hell of a time. Didn't have help enough, and she clambered all over the rocks, until we finally lost our tracking line and as she went down and out the other end. Some of us manned the oars and pulled her ashore in the small eddy. They let down from head of island a buoy with rope attached, and we pulled her up to foot of island and loaded up the outfit and pulled back to small eddy. (*Another description of crossing Grand Rapids is in "The Beaver" of March 1948, "Paris to Peel's River in 1892" by Grace Lee Nute.*) Just as we were going to bed, along came the guide and took us through the little Grand Rapids to Big Eddy, two miles below, where we tied up with the balance of the fleet.

Saturday, May 28th.

Clear. We ate Breakfast at 5:30 AM and pulled out with balance of fleet, 14 boats in all—large and small. The guide *was* at *the* head in Connor's boat. We all followed in line, one boat getting hung up shortly after the start. The fleet tied up at 10 AM and waited two hours for the other boat. When we came to a bad place, we would tie up while guide would pilot a boat through, come back and head for fleet with one of our small boats to find a channel. He took all but three boats through, only puncturing two. We tied up at head for night. A better looking country here than that above Grand Rapids.

Sunday, May 29th.

Clear. The guide will not take us through until after 3 PM, as his religion gives out at that time. Took us through all OK and we tied up while the others repaired their boats. We caught a mess of fish for supper.

Monday, May 30th.

Clear. We pulled out at 6:15 AM. Sailing was smooth until we reached the Holier (*currently called Brule or Burnt*) Rapids. At 10:30 AM we tied up and took the balance of the fleet through separate. They were bad ones, but we came through without a mishap. There are many rapids, and bad ones to, that have no name. The water is getting lower ever since we left Grand Rapids. We swamp our small boats occasionally. Asphalt (*The oil sands have been mapped and developed for crude oil extraction*) here in abundance.

Tuesday, May 31st.

Cool and cloudy. We pulled out at 6:30 AM. Went through the Drowned (*Currently called Boiler Rapids named after the HBC lost a boiler in the rapids*), Middle, Stony, and Long Rapids. They are all bad. We struck one rock in Long Rapids. We were following the guide's boat and they struck the same one. We were piloted through Stony Rapids. One of our small boats filled with water and we cut her loose. At 4 PM we tied up at head of Crooked Rapids. Guide took all but three boats through.

Wednesday, June 1st.

Cool. Breakfast at 5:20 AM. Frost last night. Guide came after us at 8:30 AM. Crooked Rapids were swift water, also very low. Good scenery. We struck once. We tied up below, and while there, Billy Clark, with seven boats, went by. (*Clark with a party of six from Toronto on board the "Nellie"*) We pulled out shortly after and overtook them, nearly all hung up at the Little Cascade. Four of our fleet were hung on Cascade and one above it. Hardly any water and only a narrow place to go through; we were close behind guide and he pointed out just the spot and we slid over OK. I went to the rescue of some of the boats that were hung up. We lined Conor's and our boats down to Big Cascade, unloaded and let them down a six foot drop and loaded up again. As usual, we had a lovely time with our skinned fingers.

Thursday, June 2nd.

Clear. We put the balance of fleet through the same performance as our own, all turning in and doing the job up quick. Had to portage about 100 feet. We pulled out between 2 and 3 o'clock and went through Mountain and Moberly Rapids; very swift. We arrived at Fort McMurray at 7:30 PM. The HBC Post is located on the high flat right hand bank. No other buildings. We shaped our cargo, so as to put up boiler and engine in AM. Wrote letters. Mosquitoes awful thick.

Friday, June 3rd.

Clear. We arose at 4 AM, made two rudders, chopped firewood, and connected boiler and engine. Took a snapshot of Steamer, Graham, pulling in to McMurry on her first trip up. (*of the year. HBC's SS Grahame, the first steamer in the Mackenzie River basin began trade in 1883.*) We pulled out at 12:30 P.M. The river is nice all along, with islands numerous. We had not gone 25 miles, when we overhauled Connors and Billie Dalztie boats, with the guide Suzie (*Cree Indian. Name appears to be a corruption of Josie or Joseph*) aboard, also Hendricks towing his two boats with his screw wheel steamer. As we passed them they kindly invited us to take a tow. We stopped to wood up and then Hendricks came along with Billy and Connors also in tow and again invited us to take a tow. We like to be agreeable, but preferred a line in front, which they finally consented to give us. After repeated attempts, Mr. Hendricks could not tighten his towline to keep out of our way. We threw it in to him and he was compelled to drop out. We gave his men orders to let go his two boats and we took Connors and Billy and went ahead. Made 50 or 60 miles. Tied up at 9PM.

Saturday, June 4th.

Cool and cloudy. We got away at 5 AM with two boats in tow. Made two short stops and tied up at 9 PM. The river's banks are picturesque and lined with wild flowers. Good channel if you can keep off the sandbars.

Sunday, June 5th.

Clear. Pulled out at 5 AM. Passed all the fleet that came through with Suzie. No more Hendricks. We are in luck to have a guide, as it is a trick to get out into Lake Athabasca. Had to feel our way single file. When we were well out in the lake, we blew a whistle and were guided in by a beacon light. Island numerous along shore. We tied up at Chippeweggan (*Fort Chipewyan*) at 1:30 AM on 6th.

Monday, June 6th.

Strong wind. Through a racket between Mrs. Braund and Miller, which occurred last night, Mr. and Mrs. Braund decided to quit party. We were until Tuesday at 9 AM trying to come to an understanding. It was decided to take Mrs. B. to Fort McPherson as a passenger, her interest in outfit, outside provisions, to pay her fare. Her husband will provide for her there and her interest in the Enterprise will stop. *(This appears to be about the time the crew found that Mrs. Braund was pregnant. In Klondike Women, Mrs. Braund reported the men did not like her cooking and threw dishes at her.)* A woman could not stand the hardships so far, and surely not what is to come. HBC Post here. *(Diary of Elizabeth Taylor quoted in "The Beaver" article in March 1948, from her trip to Ft McPherson in 1892 argues this point.)*

Tuesday, June 7th.

Cold and cloudy. Windy. This is by far the largest settlement between here and Edmonton. It is built on rocks of granite and has a large HB Post, a saw mill and some quite pretentious houses built of hewed timber, a Roman Catholic mission and school and a Church of England mission and school, also Indian tepees galore. (*Miss Taylor had documented her two hour stay and tour of the facility as, "the Hudson Bay enclosure, at each end a large warehouse of whitewashed logs, then the Factor's house, clerk's houses, blacksmith's, flag staff, observatory, all built of hewn logs. Then a long line of white houses where the employees and their families live, all on the river bank. Then the Church of England missionary's house and next to it the school house and church." Not much change in six years*) We settled our difficulties and pulled out against a head wind and current at 9:30 AM. Made one stop for wood and tied up at 11 PM. Made about 25 miles.

Wednesday, June 8th.

Cool and windy. Frost last night. Hardly any darkness, only a twilight which lasted an hour of so. (*Their location was about 150 miles south of the Arctic Circle which crosses the MacKenzie River north of Fort Good Hope. The twilight nights get shorter and become 24 hours daylight at the circle.*) Pulled out at 5 AM. (*They were on the Slave River which forms the eastern boundary of the current Wood Buffalo National Park and discharges into Great Slave Lake at Fort Resolution.*) We have aboard Mr. Frazer, brother of the Frazer at Athabasca Landing, and a NW Mounted Policeman named Trotter. We are taking them to Smith's Landing. We reached the mouth of the Peace River, shortly after our start. Strong current from here down. We arrived at Smith's Landing at 6:50 P.M. We hired Suzie to take us to Fort Smith. Price to him $20.00 and 4 oarsmen for $20.00.

Thursday, June 9th.

Clear and warm. We thought we had Suzie hired, but he came around with his cousins and demanded $20 for himself, $20 for one oarsman and 40 skins each for other three. We told him to go to Salt Creek, and tomorrow I will go down the river and see my old friend, Savayard, who is the best guide in the country. There is bad water for 16 miles—it is that far by land from here—to the fort, with a drop of 240 feet. There are three portages to make, boats and all, one of 490 yards, one 3/4 of a mile and the other over a hill a 100 feet high.

Friday, June 10th.

44 at 3 P.M. Cool, windy and a little snow. There is another way to go to Ft. Smith, to make a 20 miles portage. The HBC is charging $1.00 per hundred to take outfits over.

Saturday, June 11th.

Cold and snow. Steamer Grahame arrived about 6 AM with a few horses and oxen and a dozen Klondike outfits in tow. [*Passengers and cargo between Smith's Landing (now called Ft Fitzgerald) and Ft. Smith was by ox wagon for a 16 mile trip.*] I returned with Mr. Savayard at 2 AM. He is our guest and will guide us through next Monday. It snowed a little all day. Played the great American game of baseball and attended a concert.

Sunday, June 12th.

Snowed all day. Put in the day knocking around principal hangout, Connor's store.

Monday, June 13th.

Cool. We pulled out with four other boats and rowed 6 miles, with the exception of one stop, where we were piloted through separate. Shortly after 11 AM we reached the first portage of 490 yards. We packed out outfit over and after they all did the same, we tackled the "Enterprise" to portage her. She had to come up a steep incline, about 25 feet high. When up about 15 feet, the tackle broke. We, with the assistance of the other crew, about 25 men in all, got her over in 5 hours, with boiler and engine in.

Tuesday, June 14th.

Clear. We finished portaging boats, loaded up and started for the next portage, where we arrived at 5 PM. This consisted of three portages, boats and all, the first to a creek, about 120 yards away, which we followed for over a quarter of a mile. We then put over rocks, 10 feet high, for a distance of 100 feet, went through the creek again for a couple hundred yards and then up an incline of 100 feet, and from there a portage of 200 yards to the river. We always work from 4 to 5 AM and 10 to 12 PM. Mosquitoes terrible.

Wednesday, June 15th.

Clear. We started on small boats through the creek, which was very swift. One of them was swamped with 1000 lbs. of flour, which was all saved, and after running several more small boats through, we started the "Enterprise". This is a new way to make this portage and the channel was only from 5 to 7 feet wide in places and we had a hard time of it, digging away banks, cutting brush and falling trees. We worked hard all day, portaging boats and outfits and quit at 10:30 PM. The crowd, outside of myself, didn't sleep a wink—mosquitoes.

Thursday, June 16th.

Warm. Heavy showers at noon. We put in the time from 5 AM to 10 PM, working like braves. We loaded about 1 1/2 tons of the Lady Hamilton (*Name not listed, but a Hamilton party of 8 from Hamilton had an unnamed boat*) and our own stuff in their large canoe. When within 100 yards of Rock Portage she struck a snag which punched a hole in her middle section. She swamped and her cargo was wet before we could unload her. The worst damage was done to canoe. We also portaged quite a lot of stuff the length of the island. Some stuff was wet from rain which came on suddenly. Mosquitoes bad.

Friday, June 17th.

Clear. We were a good part of the day putting boats over last portage and loading up. We left her and had a hard pull to Mountain Portage, the last pull being across current and against heavy wind, for one hour. We reached the Mountain at 8 PM. We sized up the situation and found a hill about 120 ft. high and about 500 or 600 ft. from water to the top and a steeper ascent on the other side. A boat, as large as ours, had never gone over. We turned in early, as there was a good wind and no mosquitoes.

Saturday, June 18th.

Clear. We started early and portaged our outfit half way up the hill, taking out everything except the boiler. We washed and scrubbed her from stem to stern and found the old devil all there and not leaking a drop. We cut some skids to improve the portage. We spread out and dried the stuff, wet and on the last portage and helped some of the others portage.

Sunday, June 19th.

Clear. We were up at 5 AM and put in snubbing posts on portage, snaked out of the river some long skids and by that time the other crews were up and we all went to work portaging the boats. Our own, we tackled about 10:30 AM and put her on top of the hill before dinner, afterwards running her down to the river. The roadway was just wide enough to get her through, with a little force. By supper time we had all the boats over. After supper, we portaged our entire outfit to the boat and loaded it, winding up the job in a heavy rainstorm and going to bed good and wet at midnight.

Monday, June 20th.
Heavy rain and wind. We expected to pull out early, but were prevented by rain.

Tuesday, June 21st.
Heavy rain and wind. Called the cook at 3 AM but were fooled like, you know. One of the parties, traveling with us, consists of nine Hamilton boys. We met them about eight miles above Grand Rapids, where they concluded to stay with us good fellows.

Wednesday, June 22nd.
Heavy rain and wind. Same as the day before.

Thursday, June 23rd.
Clear. Waited for the other boats and did not get away until 7 AM. We had a hard continuous pull until 10:30 AM through all kinds of bad water and through currents, running in every direction, to a portage about a half a mile long. We only lightened two tons. We then managed the oars with 10 men and we pulled through a narrow, dangerous, rocky channel, dodging rocks on every side. Loaded up and had a hard pull of about two miles to Fort Smith, which is on left hand bank on a hill, 100 feet high. We arrived there at 4 PM. (*Fort Smith is on the border of the Northwest Territories. Miss Taylor described Ft. Smith as "4 or 5 small log houses plastered with mud ".*)

Friday, June 24th.
Rained all morning. Sid and Sam took engine to HBC shop and cleaned it. In the PM we worked, getting boat ready and raising the stern

wheel six inches. William Dalgliest *(possibly Dalgleish)* asked for a ride to Peel River, which was granted. *(The Peel was about 800 miles down stream.)* His party is going up the Laird. *(The Laird River was about 300 miles down stream at Fort Simpson)*

Saturday, June 25th.

Clear. We dried out all the provisions that were wet on portages. We put boiler and engines in place and got up steam and took a back. We received word that four HBC scows were swamped in Boiler Rapids and some mail lost. McKinley, the HBC man, has gone to Smith's Landing for the mail. We are hanging back on that account, also to get our stuff from Dr. Lyster. We heard he was in the Big Eddy June 8th.

Sunday, June 26th.

Showers. We cleaned and loaded boat, overhauled damage, and by dinner time she was in ship shape. We cut wood and steamed up and tied up to the old Wrigley *(an HBC steamer)*. We are going to tow Mr. Campbell and party, of Windsor, through with us. We pulled out at 3:30 PM, with one of our men aboard, to get some salt up Salt Creek.

Monday, June 27th.

Showers. Laid around and played cards. McKinley arrived with mail at 8 PM. We sorted all the mail, which was wet; some of the boys got letters and newspaper clippings. We pulled out at 9:15 PM and ran to Salt River, 20 miles. The Salt was too far up to go after, so we wooded up and pulled out.

Tuesday, June 28th.

Light showers. We kept going all day, only stopping for wood. The river is strewn with islands and its banks are beautiful and inviting and lined with flowers, but as soon as you pull to shore the mosquitoes jump on you and begin to chew.

Thursday, June 30th.

We steamed out at 1:30 AM. For about ten hours we went very near South. A large circle appeared around the sun, the sky turned black and the wind began to pick up. We headed for the shore and give her hell and amidst the flashes of lightning, we ran into a small bay and dropped anchor. A storm came up, which we could not have lived in.

Friday, July 1st.

Dark and stormy. West wind. We steamed out at 1:30 AM, going eight or nine miles, then we were glad to get back to a sheltered bay; we anchored and put a line to shore. A German party of 11 (*Apparently did not start at Athabasca. Some parties came overland to Lake Athebasca*) and another party of four, put in at the same bay.

Saturday, July 2nd.

Wind easy. We pulled out at 3 AM. A dead sea rolling; run 12 hours and reached the mouth of the McKenzie River. All kinds of islands. River 13 miles wide. We struck trying to get in for wood. A few hours later we anchored at the mouth of a river and picked up wood. Caught a 75lb pike with drag net. Rain storm at 7 PM, after which we pulled out.

Sunday, July 3rd.

Clear. Rain at 5 PM. We were stopped several times by rain and wind, but made a good run late at night and in the early morning of the 4th, went through rapids; must have made from 12 to 15 miles.

Monday, July 4th.

We passed Fort Providence at 2:30 AM. Made good time through a swift current, until 5 AM, when we stopped for wood. This is an elegant day, but we had a heavy rain storm at 4 PM. Later, we traded tea for moose meat. McKenzie River is a winner and about a hundred miles from mouth it narrows down with a good current.

Tuesday, July 5th.

Rain. Rained all day and night and we had to tie up.

Wednesday, July 6th.

Strong west wind. We pulled out at 5 AM. Wind blowing hard. We had consort lashed to side, but she took water so fast that we had to drop her to the stern to save her. We came in sight of Fort Simpson at 10 AM and put in shore to look over situation. The fort is located on the left hand bank at the mouth of Laird River. The wind was too hard and we had to put in opposite the fort. It calmed down, and we steamed across at 8 PM. A nice fort; reading room, library and pool table, vegetable garden and inter-ocean reporter.

Thursday, July 7th.

Warm west wind. We did a little shopping and called on Mr. Springer of Chicago; gave him an item on "Enterprise". Took on some wood, put in a new rudder post to replace one broken last night. Put in new steering gear. We hustled some vegetables. Concluded to take Mr. Campbell to mouth of Peel River. Pulled out at 2 PM and kept moving.

Friday, July 8th.

Clear. We were hung on a sand bar for two hours. The only fort at which we did not stop was Fort Wrigley, which we passed. They hoisted their flag as we passed by; it is on right hand bank and almost obscured by an island. Sun set at 10:30 PM.

Saturday, July 9th.

Clear. We stopped for wood at 5 AM. At 9 o'clock we got on gravel bar. Got off at once, but were two hours getting Campbell's boat off. We have passed seven outfits since leaving Simpson. One party had gone 10 miles past Gravel River and were tracking back. They claim a pan was washed at mouth with seven colors. They also claim that you can go up 200 miles and in two days cross to the McWilliam. Pulled into Fort Norman at 5 PM. Some of the parties here have sent men overland to prospect Gravel River. Left at 9 PM.

Sunday, July 10th.

Cloudy and windy. Wind sprang up at 5 AM and at 11 we were compelled to tie up as wind is dead ahead. Fort Norman is on right hand bank at mouth of Great Bear River. Mr. Hudson made us a map of river to Good Hope, two rapids and two ramparts. Snow on the mountains. Wind died down and we pulled out at 7 PM.

Monday, July 11th.

Clear and windy. We made the rapids and ramparts OK. Fort Good Hope is at foot of ramparts on right hand bank just below. After leaving fort, we crossed the Arctic Circle at 4:32 PM. We moved slow on account of wind.

Tuesday, July 12th.

Cloudy, rain and snow. Heavy wind. We stopped after midnight and took on a good supply of wood and pulled out as it calmed down at 1:30 AM. We tied up on account of wind at 6 AM. Pulled out again at 8 PM. We passed Grand View in evening. A stretch of river four or five miles wide and 15 long—straight.

Wednesday, July 13th.

Clear. We took on wood at noon and went through lower ramparts. At 11:30 PM we sighted the French Catholic Mission at mouth of Red River. We pulled in and got a map of channel to Fort McPherson from the priest. *(About 60 miles.)* Did a little trading with the Indians. This is the last night that the sun appears to view all night. Can see it for 44 days at McPherson.

Thursday, July 14th.

Pulled out at 1 AM and reached delta of McKenzie about 7 AM. Dropped Campbell. After going 10 miles, reached the Peel River. Passed many outfits and reached Fort McPherson at 10:15 PM. *(Confirmed in Klondike Women. Mrs. Emily Craig speaks of meeting Mrs. Braund. The Braunds left the Enterprise and joined the Craigs up the Rat River to Destruction City.)*

Friday, July 15th.

Clear. Fought mosquitoes until 3 AM and slept until noon. Mrs. B refused to get off as agreed so Sam decided to quit party. We were all day sorting out their outfits.

Saturday, July 16th.

Finished sorting out outfit. Made a copy of De Sainville's map of Peel River as far as explored by him—190 miles. *(Count E. de Sainville made this map in 1888. Copy of map in The Golden Grindstone-Adventures of George Mitchell Oxford Press 1935.)* Got up steam and pulled out at 5 PM. Run all day and night. Made Dalgliest a member of party.

Sunday, July 17th.

Clear. We ran all day and tied up at 11 PM. Passed outfit with skin boat turned over.

Monday, July 18th.

Clear. Started at 10 AM. Lined our boat through swift place. We tied up about 9:30 PM. Traveled four miles.

Tuesday, July 19th.

Warm. We pulled out at 7 AM. We tried to cross to opposite channel, but current caught us and we were in luck to get back to shore without losing much. We also tried it among the sandbars—no go. We worked around to right of sandbars and tried to cross, but were washed on a gravel bar. After hours of work, we got her off and made to where we started from. We then tried it down left hand channel—no go. We wooded up and went back among the sandbars; tried again, failed and tied up.

Wednesday, July 20th.

Warm. We put in the day bucking the currents and made a little headway.

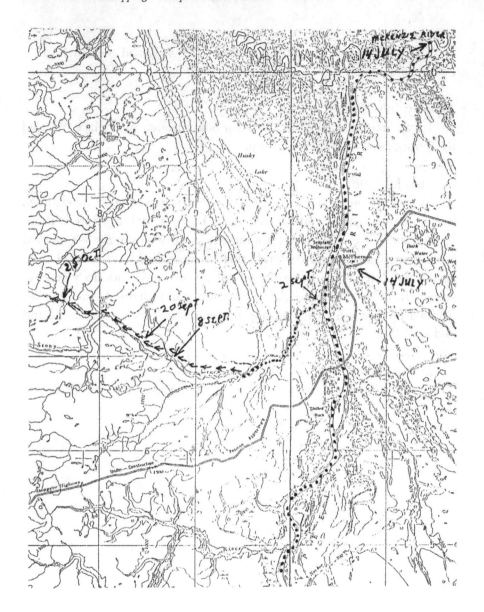

Map 5. Ft McPherson, Peel River and Stony Creek

Thursday, July 21st.
    Clear. Same as yesterday.

Friday, July 22nd.

Clear. The going ahead is getting harder each day.

Saturday, July 23rd.

Clear and cool. After repeated attempts to go ahead, we concluded we would go back a couple of miles and try left hand channel. We tried that one and tried again and seriously thought of disbanding the "Enterprise", but finally voted to go back to right hand channel. Had to use block and tackle to get there. At the place we had failed before, we tried in every conceivable shape, even lightening her a couple of tons. Worked late at night and decided to tie her up for good, leave two men with her and take seven men with two months provisions and small boats and prospect headwaters of Peel. At lottery, it fell to S. Down and L. Goermer to remain. We put up emery wheel and started to grind.

Monday, July 25th.

Spent the full day washing and mending clothes, sharpening tools, making oars and getting outfit ready.

Tuesday, July 26th.

Warm. Rain at 5 PM. We were in till 4 PM getting outfit ready and loaded. As we were eating supper, rain began to fall heavily, but it quit and we pulled out at 7:30 PM. We tracked until 11 PM, ate supper and slept on gravel bar.

Wednesday, July 27th.

Clear. Light showers. We pulled out at 10 AM, ate dinner at 3 PM and supper at 9 PM. Made 12 miles. We passed Dr. Brown's party camping ground; they are four days ahead of us.

Thursday, July 28th.

Showers. We pulled out at 11:30 AM. Hard tracking against a heavy current all day. At 3 AM we overtook Dr. Brown's party of four men and another party of two men. They left McPherson 10 days ahead of us and decided to build small boats. The only people ahead of us now are 10 men, who started from McPherson 19 days ahead of us. We put up at 9 PM and made eight miles.

Friday, July 29th.

Showers. We put out at 9:40 AM. Tracking good in some places, bad in others. Current very swift. Put out at 7:40 P.M. and made 10 miles. (*The McAdams party reported meeting part of the "Enterprise" party near the Trail River on this date. This appears to be Downs and Groemer who had remained with the "Enterprise". The McAdams diary reported that the "Enterprise" had been sold to HBC at Fort Norman.*)

Saturday, July 30th.

Showers. We pulled out at 10 AM. In the evening, one of the boats got away from us, but the other one picked it up. We put up at 8:30 PM, opposite Falling Stone. Made 12 miles.

Sunday, July 31st.

Showers. It being Sunday, we did not start till near noon and quit at 7 PM. Made eight miles.

Monday, August 1st.

Showers. We had to get up in night and cover stuff. Rain started at 9:45 AM and in two hours we were at mouth of Good Hope River. We came on to a beaver on the bar, but let him go. It was a young one. About one mile above Good Hope, we ran into a raging current, waves five feet high. High rock banks, but we track on gravel bars. Put up at 7:30 PM. Found four colors (*nuggets*). Made eight miles.

Tuesday, August 2nd.

Showers. We broke camp at 9:45 AM and turned in at 8:30 PM. Same high rock banks, 400 to 800 feet high, raging current, but eddies numerous. We did quite a bit of rowing. Made eight miles.

Wednesday, August 3rd.

Showers. Pulled out at 10:40 AM and turned in at 8:30 PM. Hard pull from start to finish. Made 10 miles.

Thursday, August 4th.

Pulled out at 11 AM. Went through ramparts and rapids and turned in at 9 PM near the mouth of Bonnet Plume River. We caught up with the other people. 3 parties in all, 10 men. Four, called the Baudette party, are from around Bay City, Mich., and all 10 are from U.S. Hard pulling. Surrounding country, mountainous.

Friday, August 5th.

Showers. The other crowd sent 7 men up the Peel to prospect and expected them back shortly, so we rested on our oars. Found two good colors opposite here. The other party went up 15 miles. We will pull out in AM.

Saturday, August 6th.

We pulled out at 10 AM and quit at 8 PM after a hot day run and camped at Indians winter camp, at foot of a sort of ramparts. Got a few colors. Made 15 miles.

Sunday August 7th

Showers. We pulled out at 10 AM and in short time were at last branch of Peel River, explored by Count De Sainville. It is the Windy River, runs south, with very swift current and large volume of water flowing out, but more riley than that of the Peel, which is as clear as crystal. We followed the river as far as the Count had explored. High rock banks and rock bottom. We climbed a hill 1000 feet high and drew a map of Peel as far as we could see, probably 123 miles. It runs west and south into the mountains. We turned at 9:30 PM at mouth of a creek on the left. Made 12 miles.

Monday, August 8th.

Rain. We arose at 8 AM and prospect the creek where we slept, also one on the right a few miles farther up. River narrowed down to 50 to 100 yards wide. Current very swift. Rock bottom and no colors. Passed some stages. Had an exciting time shooting at an animal (*Possibly a grizzly bear*). Made 15 miles.

Tuesday, August 9.

Showers. We got an early start and by noontime were as far up the Peel as anyone could get with boats. The river narrows down to 100 feet. Scenery grand beyond description. We packed up an outfit for four days and started on foot. In an hours time we were up to the wildest kinds of falls imaginable: White Horse rapids could not begin to compare with this grand canyon of the Peel. There are several continuous falls, one of 100 feet high. We put up at 8 PM made 8 miles. Went to sleep on rock banks to sound of rushing waters.

Wednesday, August 10th.

Showers. We ate slapjacks and started early. On account of the roughness of traveling and no sign of color, we concluded this would be our last day. We had to climb like mountain goats and wallow through moss to our knees. We shot 8 partridges for dinner. Made 12 miles and quit at 7:30 PM.

Thursday, August 11th.

Clear. We started for the boats. I was with Johnny and Horm. We scared up a moose and got so far from the trail that we had to put up for the night.

Friday, August 12th.

Warm rain. Went to camp early in AM and we started on return trip. At the mouth of Windy, we found a communication from Bay City boys. They went up the Windy on 10th. We made the mouth of Bonnet Plume and put up.

Saturday, August 13th,

Clear, showers. We broke camp early and put up at mouth of Good Hope River at 9 PM. We chased a beaver several miles but did not get him. Shot some loon.

Sunday, August 14th.

We pulled out and met several outfits below our camp: among them were some of the Hamilton party, which is split up. We went 2 miles up Good Hope after geese. From there down we met and talked with a good many people, in fact had a very sociable time. We had supper with Big Jim and Ernie and ran onto Mr. Campbell and Sid at 11:30 PM. They were camped with another party. We stayed all night. Our other boat made a short stop and went on a 3 AM. (*Possibly the McAdams, Huron Imisk, Idaho, Brown or Peacock parties.*)

Monday, August 15th.

Clear. We met three more parties, one the Hendricks party, and arrived at the "Enterprise" at 2:30 PM. Held a meeting in the evening and decided that E. Gautherat and JB take the "Enterprise" to McPherson and sell her, while balance of the party would build two small boats to go up the Peel. *(The Eben McAdams diary reported it caught up with the "Enterprise" group about 100 miles up the Peel near the Trail River on July 29 and that the "Enterprise" had been sold prior to this time to the Hudson Bay Company at Ft Norman.)*

Tuesday, August 16th.

Showers. We unloaded "Enterprise", sawed her down four boards, sorted out Billy's outfit as he decided to go over the Rat River. Ed and JBW. pulled out at 5 PM. *(The Rat River appears to be a tributary of the Porcupine River and located about 75 miles overland from the Peel River.)*

Wednesday, August 17th.

Clear. We got word that Billy has changed his mind about going over the Rat and has left his outfit with some Hamilton boys, a few miles below here.

Thursday, August 18th.

Clear. The boys did not return from McPherson until Wednesday, August 24th. While they were away we got our two scows built. We had to move the outfit and tent on account of rising water.

Wednesday, August 18th.

Rain. Ed, JBW and Billy arrive this AM, having sold the boat to Mr. Whittaker, the missionary. We have decided that the chances of getting over to the Stewart River on one Indian's word is very slim. We have also lost so much time that the season is too far advanced to track up Windy River, the water being too cold for the men to stand. We are therefore going back to McPherson and make a winter portage to La Pierre's House where we know there is a track. *(La Pierre's House was a trading post on the Bell River, a tributary of the Porcupine River and about 59 miles from the Peel River. It was established in 1846 on the Rat River and moved to the Bell in 1872. It was abandoned in 1893.)* JBW found out at the Fort that we had gained a day while steaming up the Peel. I have corrected it in this diary by starting properly on this day. We arrived back from our trip up the Peel on Sunday, not Monday.

Thursday, August 25th.

We loaded our boats and pulled down Peel about 12 miles and pitched camp at an eddy, where we caught fish in abundance. Our cook refused to cook for the boys.

Friday August 26th.

Every man cooks his own slapjacks on several different bonfires. We called a meeting and Miller insisted that J.B. Wright do the cooking. He would not let the party ballot and elect one and as the majority rules, and not one man, we were preparing a ballot, to "bust" or "no bust", when a compromise was made by a motion to elect 3 cooks. That was different and no cause for an election, as H. and L. Goermer and JBW volunteered to cook. We are catching all the fish we want.

Saturday, August 27th.

Clear. Went to a lake near by and shot 5 ducks, but was driven back to camp by black flies. Heavy rain at night.

Sunday, August 28th.

Clear. Did nothing but eat and sleep.

Monday, August 29th.

Clear. Same as yesterday. We will pull out tomorrow.

Tuesday, August 30th.

Light showers. Pulled out a 9:30 AM and tied up at 7 PM. Caught 4 fish.

Wednesday, August 31st.

Clear. Pulled out at 11 AM and tied up at 7 PM. Heavy wind late at night, also rain. Darkness sets in before 9 PM.

Thursday, September 1st.

Rain at night. We run 8 hours, put up on a sandbar, opposite Indian camp.

Friday, September 2nd.

Clear. Pulled out at 7 AM. Both scows and a canoe using sails. Fair wind and good sport. At 3 PM we pulled into the mouth of Little Nell Creek, where starts the winter portage. We found the Toronto boys camped there. We had been looking for them. We pitched our camp next to theirs. Heavy rain all night.

Saturday, September 3rd.

Rain all day. I went hunting with one of the Toronto boys and got 7 ducks. An old Californian by the name of Brown pulled in this afternoon. We invited him to supper and a bed in our tent which he accepted.

Sunday, September 4th.

Clear. Some of the boys went to Fort to attend church. Shot a few ducks from tent door. Ice formed on water left in wash basin last night.

Monday, September 5th.

Clear, rain at night. Went duck shooting in afternoon. We got 11 ducks and caught an 8 pound salmon trout in gill net—a beautiful fish.

Tuesday, September 6th.

Warm. Water raised enough last night to float one of our scows off and into the Peel. English "Bobby" picked her up.

Wednesday, September 7th.

Clear. Sid and I went shooting. Got 12 ducks, Billy, Johnny and Herm helped Brown up the creek with his outfit. They did not return at night.

Thursday, September 8th.

Windy. The boys returned from up creek at 9:30 PM. They took Brown up about 8 miles and claim we can take 1200 pounds that far in a scow.

Friday, September 9th.

Windy. Seven of us went to McPherson to get our tent from Braund. He refused to give it up and a wrangle, we took it.

Saturday, September 10th.

We left H. Goermer at camp to cook. We went up the creek with two scows, loaded with 122 pounds each. We left camp at 8 AM and arrived 8 miles up at 12:30 and rowed all the way back, making the return trip in 2 1/2 hours. We tracked only a small part of the way, rowing the balance. The further up you go, the swifter it gets. Frost at night.

Sunday, September 11th.

Clear. We left camp at 8 AM. Made same time as yesterday. Toronto boys took a load up to within 2 1/2 miles of us.

Monday, September 12th,

Cold. Rained mostly all day. Laid up account of rain.

Tuesday, September 13th.

Cold, light showers. We got away at 10 AM, with the two scows loaded with the balance of our outfits, making two rather heavy loads and as the water had raised 6 inches, the current is swifter and it made rather hard work. The first boat arrived at 5 PM. We put up tent and rolled in.

Wednesday, September 14th.

Cloudy, rain. Did nothing today.

Thursday, September 15th.

Cloudy. Light showers. We improved our sleeping apartments. J. Block went to McPherson and traded oil for moccasins.

Friday, September 16th.

Clear. Did nothing.

Saturday, September 17th.

Cool. Snowed in evening. Four of us took 1000 pounds of provisions about three miles up the creek in a scow, while JBW overhauled the pork and bacon and found it in good condition.

Sunday, September 18th.

Cool. Snowed all day and last night.

Monday, September 19th.

Clear. We wrangled with each other as to the best way and time to get over the trail. Toronto boys returned the scow we loaned them. We let them take canoe.

Tuesday, September 20th.

Clear. Below freezing last night. Snow tonight. We held a meeting in the morning and decided to build a shack in the spruce timber half a mile from here and to live there until spring. But, in the meantime, to portage on the first half what we do not require here, as far over as we can get. Started on shack.

Wednesday, September 21st.

Snow at night. We got the walls of the shack completed today. Inside dimensions 16X22.

Thursday, September 22nd.

Light snow. Cold. Worked on shack in afternoon. Dark 6:30 P.M.

Friday, September 23rd.

Snow. We worked on shack.

Saturday, September 24th.

Clear. J. Block and H. Goermer went to McPherson for mail and returned at 7:30 PM without any.

Sunday, September 25th.

Clear. Laid up today.

Monday, September 26th.

Snow. Worked on shack.

Tuesday, September 27th.

Snow. Worked on shack.

Wednesday, September 28th.

We have to carry stones for fireplace from the creek 200 yards distance, and for good clay, a half mile down the creek—one mile from here—carry it a half mile.

Thursday, September 29th.
Snow.

Friday, September 30th.
Snow. Worked on shack.

Saturday, October 1st.
Clear. We moved into shack. Billy and J. Block went for mail. Did not arrive.

Sunday, October 2nd.
Clear. We fixed up the camp. One year ago yesterday the thermometer at McPherson registered 7 degrees below zero.

Monday, October 3rd.
Cloudy. Put in a quiet day. Sid and JBW shot 18 muskrats and we ate them.

Tuesday, October 4th.
Cloudy. L. Goermer, Billy, Sid and I started to build toboggans.

Wednesday, October 5th.
Clear. We continued to work on toboggans. It is understood Billy is going over this fall. Herm and Lew talk the same way.

Thursday, October 6th.
Worked on toboggans.

Friday, October 7th.
Snow. There is a great deal of dissatisfaction in the party. Miller and Ed will listen to nothing, but go in the Spring. Rather than have a continual wrangle, I have decided to go over with Sid, Johnny and JBW as soon as possible.

Saturday, October 8th.
    Worked on sleigh.

Sunday, October 9th.
    Clear. Put in all day on toboggans.

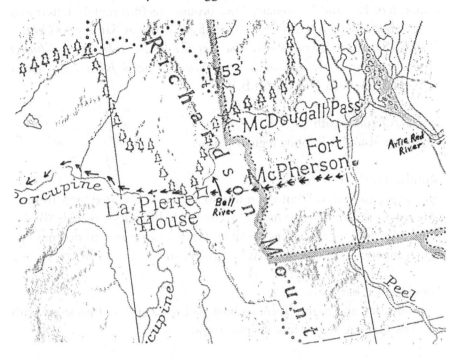

Map 6. Ft. McPherson to La Pierre House and down the Porcupine River

Monday, October 10th.
    Worked on toboggans, About zero tonight.

Tuesday, October 11th.
    Put out a few snares.

Wednesday, October 12th.
    Zero, clear. Set 17 more snares, some as far as three miles away.

Thursday, October 13th.
    2 below zero. Sid and I went to visit Toronto boys.

Friday, October 14th.

Clear. Rabbits went around snares galore.

Saturday, October 15th.

J. Block and Billy brought mail from McPherson. Scow was frozen in at mouth of Peel and McKenzie. They brought us (not me) 44 letters and some papers. We got word of Gen. Shafter's battle at Santiago. (*General Shafter's Battle for Santiago de Cuba was fought 2-6 July 1898. Admiral Sampson destroyed the Cuban fleet off Santiago on 3 July.*) Also, got a miniature American Flag from J.B.W.

Sunday, October 16th.

Storm at night. Rabbits regularly now.

Monday, October 17th.

Stormed at night. Went the round of snares. Was visited by 3 Toronto boys and in the evening we held a meeting. All difficulties settled. We will all go over the trail as soon as possible. H. & L. Goermer to do cooking. When anyone drops out of party, he will get an equal share of everything.

Tuesday, October 18th.

Snow day and night. Toronto boys will make a start tomorrow with 100 Lbs. each. Almost a foot of light snow.

Wednesday, October 19th.

Clear, stormy at night. We dug up our snares and in afternoon JBW and myself went up creek in search of Ptarmigans. On our return trip, about 1 1/2 miles from camp, we met Alf Davidson. He was fagged out and did not think he could make camp. I put my gun on his toboggan. JBW did the same and I told him to get on and I would pull him (Alf). We had not gone far when JBW's gun went off and nearly took a finger off Alf's left hand. We got him to camp and Sid dressed the wound. Ed, Johnny and Charlie, of the Springfield party, made an attempt to cross the Peel and get a doctor but could not make it. The balance of the Toronto party were all pretty much played out and straggled along at all hours.

Thursday, October 20th.

Light snow all day and night. Sid and I went to McPherson and returned with Dr. Lang who dressed Alf's hand and found the bone of one finger broken. Can save the finger.

Friday, October 21st.

Light snow all day. We were visited by a man named Bell from Rat River. He is going out to Dawson City in a few days; will carry mail and bring back information. Will charge one dollar per head.

Saturday, October 22nd.

Clear. 20 degrees below zero. Ed, Billy and Johnny went to the fort with doctor; bought a stove.

Sunday, October 23rd.

24 below zero. Frank Davison collected letters for Bell to deliver at Fort. While there he secured a room at the missionaries for Alf who will stay there for six weeks or until his hand is well. Frank will continue on the trip with the boys.

Monday, October 25th.

11 below at 9 PM. Mr. Firth delivered our stove with a dog team; he also took the canoe for which he gave Billy $30.00. Some of us pulled our first toboggan load to waterhole—100 lbs. We will pull 5 miles tomorrow.

Tuesday, October 25th.

23 below. We all pulled out at 7 AM and were back before 10 AM. After dinner we loaded 150-160 lbs. and pulled to water hole.

Johnny froze his nose.

Wednesday, October 26th.

24 below. We made two trips, all of us except Billy and Ed who went to the Fort with the intention of buying a dog team to take them to Fort Yukon. They cannot stand the idea of working so hard and Ed is afraid of freezing to death.

Thursday, October 27th.

Windy. We all made one trip with the exception of Billy and Ed who again went to McPherson. We loaded and pulled to water hole.

Friday, October 28th.

20 below. Ed bought the missionary's dog team for $130.00, the full amount of the note we held against him for "Enterprise". They will be delivered tomorrow. We made two trips today. Sid and JBW went through 3 1/2 miles beyond the cache and pitched big tent—good shelter—good wood.

Saturday, October 29th.

20 below. We made a trip to cache but concluded we would live in shack until Monday. Ed and Billy arrived with dog team, all 21 dogs, good harness and toboggan, a Whittager missionary and an Indian named Davis to guide them over the mountain. They will pull out Monday.

Sunday, October 30th.

Most of the boys are suffering with a bad cold. Wrote letter today.

Monday, October 31st.

We broke camp and pulled through to our tent where we will live until further notice. Sid and I took up the rear, took out windows, etc. Ed and Billy pulled out this AM. Mr. Stone, the doctor (*Dr Lyster*) and party went by on their return from La Pierre's House. They were hungry.

Tuesday, November 1st.

I made a trip to shack to pick up stuff left behind. There is still a load left at shack.

Wednesday, November 2nd.

Nine dog teams, with fish from La Pierre's House passed our camp before 8 AM. JBW went through to shack for load. The balance of us made two trips. Sid sick—layed off half day. The Indians brought a note from Ed. They laid up at foot of mountains with a sick dog; they say the distance is 30 miles from our tent.

Thursday, November 3rd.

We all made two trips with the exception of Sid who is sick.

Friday, November 4th.

We all made two trips. Indians went by on their return trip. A Porcupine River Indian, named William Husky, says there are 40 men at Old Crow River digging; 430 more at Black River near Fort Yukon. Crow River is about 140 miles from here—was he talking for a meal? That is the question.

Saturday, November 5th.

Some of us on the pull 3 1/2 miles above here. Van Natta, Bob Smith and Mr. Brown are camped there. Mr. Brown decided to try it this fall and is traveling with Van and Bob.

Sunday, November 6th.

Windy. We worked only a half day.

Monday, November 7th.

Wind blew hard last night and made the trip hard pulling. Made two trips. Names of Toronto outfit: Frank Davison, Alfred Davison, at Fort; Jack Par, Arthur Reinboden, Thomas Moody, William Henry, Charles Smith; other people on trail—Robert Brown, Robert Smith, Frank Van Natta, James Wilson, James MacDermand.

Tuesday, November 8th.

We made two trips. Will break camp in AM.

Wednesday, November 9th.

We arose early and made 2 1/2 miles above our cache. Good wood—good shelter.

Thursday, November 10th.

Made two loads.

Friday, November 11th.

Two trips about 200lbs each.

Saturday, November 12th.

About 3 inches of snow fell last night which made the pulling hard, but we cleaned up the cache and now have everything up to the tent.

Sunday, November 13th.
    Put in day mending and resting.

Monday, November 14th.
    It having snowed for the last few days, the trail was in bad shape in AM and we could only wiggle with 100lbs, in PM regular load.

Tuesday, November 15th.
    We each made two good loads.

Wednesday, November 16th.
    Same

Thursday, November 17th.
    Storming with high west wind. Too stormy to work. Four loaded dog teams through to La Pierre's House. We traded tea for about 30 lbs. venison; Toronto boys game. Indians went on, wind to their backs.

Friday, November 18th.
    Stormed same as yesterday.

Saturday, November 19th.
    Where the wind had struck the creek it laid the ice bare. L. Goermer and JBW went 1 1/2 miles beyond cache, near mouth of a creek and selected camping site and cut wood. Sid went scouting ahead and Van Natta to locate the last timber this side of the mountains where we could build a shack. They report 7 miles above our cache as the place. We would have pulled further today but supposed we were at the last timber.

Sunday November 20th.
    We moved today. The Indians, on their return trip, stopped in with a note from Mr. Firth (*HBC post manager*), telling of Ed and Billy's safe arrival at La Pierre's House and their departure from there in good order. David also dropped in today from the other direction with a letter from Ed. They say the mountain is a terror; they had to make two trips of their

load. The trail on the other side of the mountain is very bad with a big drop off and they followed a creek for only six miles. They advise us to get as far as we can but not to attempt to cross this year.

Monday, November 21st.
    Made two loads each.

Tuesday November 22nd.
    Snow at night. Made 3 loads each.

Wednesday, November 23rd.
    We cleaned up cache and pulled 2 1/2 miles further up. Alf Davison came up for some medicine—hand doing nicely. A band of hungry Indians pitched their teepees along side our camp. They are from Peel River.

Thursday, November 24th.
    Ten below. Thanksgiving day. We each made one trip. We had three guests for dinner, Mr. Brown, Smith and Van Natta. Had roast venison, plum duff and mince pie.

Friday, November 25th.
    Pulled two loads.

Saturday, November 26th.
    Sid and I, with some of the Toronto boys, went to pick a camping spot. We also intended to get wood but we were glad to get back to Van's tent as Sid froze his nose and fingers and nipped my toes. The balance of the party made two loads. Johnny Block froze his cheeks.

Sunday, November 27th.
    We laid in.

Monday, November 28th.
    49 below. We each made one load.

Tuesday, November 29th.
    We moved today. Miller, J. Block and I went ahead.

Wednesday, November 30th.

I was appointed to look up a site for a shack and did so on the left side of the creek 50 yards back in the timber. The others pulled up loads. Miller, J. Block and I were picked to build shack while L. Goermer, Sid and JBW pulled up outfit.

Thursday, December 1st.

We are building in connection with the Toronto boys, each one 14X16 inside. Ptarmigans are plentiful. Daylight at 8:50 AM and darkness at 3 PM.

Friday, December 2nd.

JBW., Sid and L.G. appointed on wood committee. They helped us carry big logs today. Six dog teams passed on way to La Pierre's House. L. Miller went to bed, complaining of cramps in his stomach.

Saturday, December 3rd.

Wind and snow at night. Did our regular work. Miller awoke with cramps in stomach and rheumatism in his legs.

Sunday, December 4th.

We did no work. Miller no better.

Monday, December 5th.

Trail bad today. We all carried logs. In AM Miller is no better. We wait on him.

Tuesday, December 6th.

Dog teams stopped on their way from La Pierre's House. Miller still in bad shape. I made him a pair of crutches.

Wednesday, December 7th.

Warm wind from northwest. It thawed all day and rained half the time, freezing at night. We still get enough birds to get a few meals ahead.

Thursday, December 8th.

High NW wind. We did the regular thing.

Friday, December 9th.

The trail was in good shape today and the boys brought 300 lbs. each. Miller no better.

Saturday, December 10th.

Eight or ten inches of snow fell and blocked trail. We worked on shack. Mr. Brown paid us a visit. Miller slightly improved.

Sunday, December 11th.

No work today. Went shooting and got 13 birds. Miller better.

Monday, December 12th.

We have killed 60 birds today and have more than half that number on hand. Miller better.

Tuesday, December 13th.

Wind and snow in AM. The Sleigh gang got 15, 75.

Wednesday, December 14th.

We did our regular work, besides getting 10 birds. 85.

Thursday, December 15th.

Sid and I took a shotgun each and went up the creek for a couple of days hunt. I slept with Jimmy and Mack Brown while Sid stopped with Van and Bob.

Friday, December 16th.

Snow. We took a trip up to Brass House. The trail up in this locality is a fright. I got 9 birds, which we gave to the boys up here and returned home.

Saturday, December 17th.

We did regular work.

Sunday, December 18th.

Put finishing touches on shack. Miller still in bad shape.

MISSING DIARY ENTRIES 19 Dec to 8 Feb.

Thursday, February 9th.

Mending pants most all day. Herman and John making mitts.

Friday, February 10th.

Indians came from Fort with dog teams bound for La Pierre's House. They told us that some moose were down the valley about 9 miles; we started down and saw where they had been about a week ago, so we came back tired out.

Saturday, February 11th.

Mending pants all day.

Sunday, February 12th.

Sewing on wooden buttons on pants and packing my dunnage.

Monday, February 13th.

J.B. Wright, Sid Down, J. Block, H. Goermer and myself went up Big Hill, put up tent and cut wood.

Tuesday, February 14th.

Six of us went up to the Big Hill and pulled up half of our stuff. Five dog teams stopped at our cache for the night.

Wednesday, February 15th.

Went up to Big Hill and pulled up remainder of our stuff. Husky dogs got in our cache and ate about 60lbs of our bacon. Had great sport. Riding down hill, one of the Toronto boys' toboggan got out of the track and ran into a tree nearly breaking his leg.

Thursday, February 16th.

Didn't do anything today.

Friday, February 17th.

Mending moccasins most all day. Six birds.

Saturday, February 18th.

Pulled a load up the Big Hill. A man, named Greg, stopped here over night on hid way to La Pierre's House with dog team, from Rat River. He reports 3 men dead and 11 down sick with scurby. 255 birds with today's shoot.

Sunday, February 19th.

Passed the day quietly. Had last dinner out in shack. Had plum duff and birds; for supper we had canned corn and chocolate. It's the last until we get over the mountains. *(No more canned goods.)*

Monday, February 20th.

Intended to move this morning but the wind started to blow and its blowing a hurricane yet and its getting colder.

Tuesday, February 21st.

Milder. Wind is still blowing. Started at noon and got to the foot of Big Hill in time for supper.

Wednesday, February 22nd.
All hands pulled 100 lbs. 6 miles. It was a nice clear day but cold.

Thursday, February 23rd.
We all made a load each.

Friday, February 24th.
Six loads went up the line. I am nearly knocked out with a lame knee tonight.

Saturday, February 25th.
All hands went up the line and came back tired. Trail drifted full. Stove nearly blinds us with smoke. It got too bad and play "freezeout". Living in a tent when its 40 or 50 below zero is no fun.

Sunday, February 26th.
Went up to our upper cache; hauled 3 loads of wood 3 miles to our last camping place. J.B. Wright, H. Goermer and Frank Davison started back little too late; got half way up Big Hill and nearly froze. Their faces froze in bad shape and were as white as snow when they came in. The wind is howling and it's most awful cold; can hardly keep warm in the tent. Its a dire case of freezeout this night when the fire goes out.

Monday, February 27th.

Started out and thought we would have to turn back. Froze my cheek and nose. The boy's faces are as black as my old hat.

Tuesday, February 28th.

Did not go out today, too cold. Hard wind blowing. Going to bed with clothes on—all I got. My overcoat too small to go over all my clothes, so will put it on top bed.

Wednesday, March 1st.

Pulled up camp at 8:30 AM. Had a hard day of it. Some of the boys bushed. Did not get into camp until 9:40 PM.

Thursday, March 2nd.

All of us went to top of summit, except Sid and J.B. It's a hard pull. We started with 50lbs on our toboggan and found it could be bettered by putting on 100lbs.

Friday, March 3rd.

All hands took a load up to summit.

Saturday, March 4th.

Wind blowing hard. Did not go out. Four Indians stopped here on their way to Fort.

Sunday, March 5th.

All went to the top with 100lbs. Nice day. Sun shone most of day.

Monday, March 6th.

All made load today.

Tuesday March 7th.

Colder and wind blowing some. All went up with a load. J.B. froze his nose on his way home, in bad shape.

Wednesday, March 8th.

Could not go out today. Wind blowing most awful hard and cold; cannot keep warm in tent today. Sometimes it seems as tent and all would go up with the wind. Run short of wood in PM. Burnt some of our extra toboggans. Wind let up toward evening. Gave us time to rustle some dry willows.

Thursday, March 9th.
Took last of stuff to top of summit. Wind blowing hard this evening.

Friday, March 10th.
Pulled up tent at 7:30. Toronto boys helped us to the top of summit and some of them helped us over the falls. Wind in our favor, blowing hard in our back. This is our longest move—15 miles.

Saturday, March 11th.
Could not go out today: Wind too cold.

Sunday, March 12th.
We went over to the other side and helped the Toronto boys over summit and falls.

Monday, March 13th.
Went up to the summit. Could not get a load. Some of us got to cache but could not tie on our loads, too cold. Wind blowing at a great rate. All had to come back 7 miles. J.B. on sick list.

Tuesday, March 14th.
What a difference there is between this morning and one year ago. All of us went up to summit but J.B. We pulled all of our stuff down to the foot of falls. Falls is a 35 ft drop. Lew Goermer fell and broke his arm.

Wednesday, March 15th.
Hauled five loads to tent. Lew feeling easy.

Thursday, March 16th.
Stuff all down to tent except three loads.

Friday, March 17th.

St Patrick's Day. Thanksgiving day for us. We had this day for rest. We had the best we had for dinner. It's a great satisfaction to know that we are over the mountains at last. Got 34 birds this afternoon.

Saturday, March 18th.
The boys went down the line with a load. I went hunting and got 37 birds.

Sunday, March 19th.
Hunting in the morning. 15 birds.

Monday, March 20th.
Moved camp 9 miles. It was the hardest pull we have had. The water was over the ice in too many places; lots of springs keep bursting out. Toboggans would freeze on bottom and pull like a ton. We all got our feet good and wet.

Tuesday, March 21st.
Did not work; Wind blowing hard.

Wednesday, March 22nd.
Made two trips. Nice day. No water on ice.

Thursday, March 23rd.
Made one trip. Wind blowing and drifting.

Friday, March 24th.
Did not go out.

Saturday, March 25th.
Two trips. Fine day.

Sunday, March 26th.
One trip. Nice day.

Monday, March 27th.
One trip except one of the boys. He went back to get a load that was left behind. Got in the water and came back empty.

Tuesday, March 28th.
Made three loads to foot of last hill. Wind blowing.

Wednesday, March 28th.
Moved camp for the last time. Nice weather, sun out all day.

Thursday, March 30th.
Sid and Van hauling deer (*Possible caribou*). Four dog teams passed on trail bound for the port. (*La Pierre's house*)

Friday, March 31st.
Did not do very much today. Getting ready to divide up. There is one in the party we have to get rid of—it's a redheaded guy by the name of Miller.

Saturday, April 1st.
Did not do much.

Sunday, April 2nd.
Spent the day quietly.

Monday, April 3rd.
Commenced dividing up.

Tuesday, April 4th.
Finished dividing at noon. Alf Davison and myself started for the Porcupine. Stopped at the La Pierre House the first night.

Wednesday, April 5th.
Second night, within six miles of the Porcupine. Got my feet wet and froze them both.

Thursday, April 6th.
Found that we could not haul our stuff to the Porcupine so made up our minds to stop here and build boats.

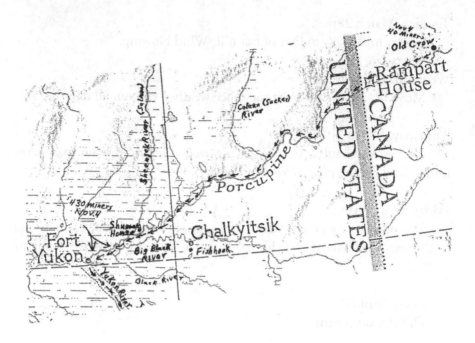

Map 7. Porcupine River to Old Crow, Rampart House to Ft Yukon

Friday, April 14th.
    Got a lot of fresh meat.

Wednesday, April 19th.
    Started for the Rat River. Stopped at La Pierre House over night.

Thursday, April 20th.
    Started with three Indians this morning. Got out about four spells. (*Rest periods*) Stopped at Indian teepee and had dinner. Started out on trail once more. Got to McLaren's shack at about 9 PM. Had supper and stayed over night.

Friday, April 21st.
    Got to the miner's camp at noon; had a good time. I got acquainted with a good many from Athabasca Landing.

Saturday, April 22nd.

Stayed around there all day. They held a miner's meeting on one of the miners and took all his stuff from him.

May 29th.

Broke camp at 5 PM and made portage over 200 feet of ice, boats and all. At the next bad place, there was a winding ten foot channel through ice seven foot thick. Water very swift. Johnny and I made an attempt to go through and were swamped. Lucky to get out of hole. Our stuff was wet but we saved it. Put up to eat at midnight.

May 30.

Kept going ahead and put up to camp at 4 AM. Started again at noon. Rough water and sharp turns. Reached the Bell River. Went a few miles. Met ice jam and broke it. It jammed several times but force of water behind it carried it out. Drifted about 5 miles and met another jam. Camped.

May 31st.

Arrived at La Pierre's House at 3 AM. Fired a salute and sung a song. Stopped and said goodbye. Made a few miles and was stopped by a big ice jam.

June 1st.

Passed three rivers and reached the Porcupine River at 7:30 PM. Stopped at Indian camp. There were 12 boats in line. The La Pierre House Push following us out. We pulled across the river and put up to cook. Started about 11:30 PM with five boats lashed together. Swift current. Strong wind.

June 2nd.

Made Old Crow at 11 PM. (*Old Crow, Yukon Territory, Canada, where Old Crow River enters the Porcupine River.*) Put up to sleep and wait for better weather.

June 3rd.

Pulled out at 6:30 AM. Good sailing all day. Went through ramparts and rapids. Swift current. Fine scenery. Reached Ramparts House (*Old Rampart, Alaska. On the Porcupine River where the Rapid River enters the*

Porcupine) at 5:30 PM. Met miners that came from Dawson (*Dawson City, Yukon Territory, Canada. About two hundred miles up the Yukon River*) to prospect. Stopped all night. To go down with them in AM.

June 4th.

We pulled out late in AM. Jack Rae seen a bear (*Probably a grizzly bear*). Fun all night. Sixty miles off Ramparts (*Old Rampart*).

June 5th.

River full of islands. (*Near mouth of Sheenjak River*) A great many channels. Bad head wind.

June 6th.

Bad day all around. Alf Davison accidentally shot himself through arm and leg with shotgun. Sid dressed the wounds and Frank, Jack Rae and myself put him in my boat and started for Fort Yukon which we made in less than 6 hours, a distance of about 30 miles. We took him to the Episcopal Mission House. Minister redressed the wounds and, as good luck would have it, along came a steamer, Straton, and minister (*Possibly Peter Trimble Rowe, Episcopal bishop of Alaska*) took him to Circle City (*Circle, Alaska*) to hospital.

June 7th.

Boys got in today. Sid and Jack lost boat and all. Also, Lou and Horm Goermer lost theirs with most of my provisions. We all unloaded and moved into a shack.

June 11, 1899.

To keep this diary required a great deal of time and pains and, after the reverses of the last few days, I think it will take me all my time to keep myself, hence this conclusion:

Since I have left Detroit I have used my best endeavors, poor as they are, to keep a correct account of all the most important events of this trip. There is a great deal more between the lines than is written down and a reference to almost any day when we were on the go would furnish a story that would fill this book. As to whether or not our trip was a failure is a question. We are in the same boat with thousands of others. We took a route which was advertised to be a good one and, to a person on the outside, looked feasible. But since we have reached Fort Yukon where we can converse with people who have come in from all the different routes, we find that any other is a pleasure trip compared to the way we came. Therefore, we consider ourselves in luck that we are here at all. We came through a country that was supposed to be good territory in which to look for the yellow metal and did also abound with game. We do not know anyone who has been successful as regards to gold nor did weslaughter a lot f game but have had the opportunity to do a great deal of trading for meat with the Indians which made our outfit last out. The only riches I have gained has been in experience and satisfaction of meeting with and surmounting difficulties of which there were many. We had the pleasure of successfully coming through a succession of bad waters for obstructions to navigation the world has no equal. We also have the credit of bringing the first steamboat thru for Athabasca Landing to Fort McPherson, Peel River. We were received at all different Posts (*Hudson's Bay Company posts*) with surprise at our being on earth as many old heads had expected us to come to grief in many places. After going up the Peel River as far as the steamboat could cope with the swift currents we took boats and went on a prospecting trip, pulling our boats thru raging currents, ramparts and rapids, until we came to impassable barriers in the shape of gigantic falls whose beauty would quicken the heart of any nature lover. From there we walked two days further up than any white man had ever been until we were satisfied that there was nothing there for us. We went up the Peel to look for gold. We did not find any but on our way back we met over a hundred men going up to take the same chance of getting over the Rockies and into the head waters of the Stewart River. We considered it too long a chance or impossible and it was lucky for us that we so decided as we interviewed people today who arrived from the first steamer from Dawson City. We find that many a poor fellow has left hisbones in that locality. Dr. Brown, who left Fort McPherson with ten men, has arrived at Dawson with two, the others having starved or frozen to death.

After coming down the Peel River our next move was to get west of the Rockies with our outfit. We were too late to attempt the summer portage and Mr. Firth, the BC manager (*John Firth was post manager from 1893 to 1920*), said we could not pull by hand over the water trail. We had learned by experience that what the HBC fogies did not know of the capabilities of intelligent white men would fill a large size book, so we set to work to do another trick never performed by white men. The distance from McPherson to La Pierre's House is 62 miles as the crow flies and about 85 miles by trail. We pulled our outfit to a creek four miles from McPherson. Then we built a shack on ground that was virtually a cake of ice. We also built a large fireplace and the more fires we built the harder time we had to keep it from sinking through to China. We built 15 toboggans and, in October, we started to pull over the trail. Before the first of December we had knocked off 26 miles more. We then put up another shack where we put in a fairly good time for a couple months. We located in a good place for hunting ptarmigan and I killed a great many. We always had plenty to eat. They are a good preventative for scurby.

On February 21st we quit the shack and started over the mountain this time making 44 miles to within 8 miles of La Pierre's House on the Shoot River. Pulled 70 miles in all.

On our first trip in November the thermometer at McPherson reached 42 below zero. In the latter part of February it went down to 58 below but was supposed to be 5 to 10 degrees colder in the mountains. We lived in an 8 ounce duck tent but did not suffer much. We reached the Shoot River April 1st and built boats. From there to Fort Yukon we took more chances than the boys who went to Cuba.

We hear that the Klondike is as rich as it ever was reported to be but there have been no new finds of any importance and the lucky members who staked first are immensely rich and the others are becoming poorer. From all reports the Canadian officials are worse than the most corrupt and it is impossible to stake a claim where there is a possible chance of there being any gold. We have done some tall hustling in the past few days to get enough grub to live on.

On Saturday we chopped and carried to the bank, a distance of over a quarter mile, three cords of wood which we sold for $18 worth of grub. That was all we could get rid of as the market is glutted with wood. We have several more strings to pull but the future does not look exceedingly bright. We are living with the Toronto boys who are sharing with us. We have the satisfaction of knowing who our friends are and that we are in God's country under the protection of Old Glory.

Signed—Otto Lahser
June 11, 1899

Who is Who

Baudette party	4 from Bay City on Peel
Bell	Man from Rat R.
Block, Jack or Johnny	Enterprise member
"Brass House"	Unknown. Probably a trading post.
Braund, Sam & Mrs.	Enterprise members
Brown, Dr Robert	Party of 4 on Peel. Left overland for Dawson with ten and arrived with 2
Campbell, Capt	Windsor party
Clark, Billy	6 from Toronto on "Nellie"
Connors, Billy	From Edmonton. At Ft Smith trading post
Dalztie, Billy	Party
Dalgliest, William	Late joining Enterprise member
Davidson, Alf	Toronto party
Davis	Native guide Ft. McPherson
Davison, Frank	Toronto party
de Sainville, Count	Explorer. Mapped Peel R. 1888
Down, Sid	Enterprise member
"Dr Lyster"	Boat of the Lyster party
"Enterprise"	Boat and group name
Firth, John	HBC mgr. Ft. McPherson
Fraser	Athabasca Landing
Frenchmen	stranded group

Gautherat, Ed	Enterprise member
"Grahame"	HBC steamship
Goermer, Horm	Enterprise member
Goermer, L.	Enterprise member
Hamilton Boys	8 from Hamilton, Ont.
HBC	Hudsons Bay Company
Hendricks	Fargo party & steamer
Henry,	William Toronto party
Hudson	HBC man at Ft Norman
Huron	Imisk Party on Peel R.
Idaho	Party on Peel R.
"La Pierre's House"	HBC post on Bell R.
"Lady Hamilton"	Boat of Hamilton party
Lahser, Otto	Principal character
Lang, Dr.	FT McPherson
Leitch, George T.	Minneapolis. Owned "Sparrow"
Lyster, Dr	Dr W.J. Lister. Detroit group. Owned
"Dr Lyster"	
MacDermand, James	On Peel R.
McAdams, Eben	Party on Peel R.
McKinly	HBC man at Ft Smith
Miller, Louis	Enterprise member
Moody, Thomas	Toronto party
"Nellie"	Boat of Billy Clark
Par, Jack	Toronto party
Peacock	Party on Peel
Potter	Edmonton
Reinboden, Arthur	Toronto party
Rowe, Peter T.	Episcopal bishop
Savayard	Cree guide

Short, Capt	Cree guide, Louis Fousseneuve, AKA Captain Shott or Captain Shot. Guide on Grand Rapids
Smith, Billy	Group on Athabasca R.
Smith, Charles	Toronto party
Smith, Robert	On Peel R.
"Sparrow"	Boat of George Leitch
Springer	Reporter at Ft Simpson
Suzie	Name corruption of Joseph or Josie. Cree guide at Fort McMurry
Savayard	Ft Smith
Sweeper Man	Unidentified party
Toronto outfit:	Frank Davison, Alfred Davison, Jack Par, Arthur Reinboden, Thomas Moody, William Henry, Charles Smith
Trotter	RCMP officer
Van Natta, Frank	On Peel R.
Whittaker	Missionary at Ft McPherson
Wilson, James	On Peel R.
Winnipeg Boys	Any of 3 groups from Winnipeg
"Wrigley"	HBC steamer
Wright, J. B.	Enterprise member

Bibliography

Grahe, Angus. The Golden Gringdstone—Adventures of George Mitchell related by Angus Grahe. Oxford Press 1935.

MacGregor, J.G., The Klondike Rush Through Edmonton, 1897-1898

Mayer, Melanie J. Klondike Women—True Tales of the 1897-98 Gold Rush. Swallow Press, Ohio University Press

McAdams, Eben. trip diary

Nute, Grace Lee. "The Beaver" Mar 48. "Paris to Peel's River in 1892". Taylor, Elizabeth. Diary of trip to Ft McPherson

Webb, Melody. Yukon, the Last Frontier. U. Nebraska Press, 1993.

My Uncle's Cabin

Uncle Otto went north
By the backdoor route in the spring of '98
Down the MacKenzie and the Porcupine
And up the Yukon to confront his fate.

In September the group built a cabin
Near the Peel on Little Nell Creek.
It housed eight burly prospectors
And measured 16 X 22 feet.

For a winter trek to La Pierre's House
They made sleds and lots of snow shoes.
The built another cabin in November
Near the treeline where the winter was blue.

The trek was over in March '99
Then canoes down the Bell and the Crow.
They reached Ft. Yukon in June of that year
And still had a long way to go.

He headed south in '02 with a poke full of gold.
With adventure, he'd had his fill.
"We took more chances than the boys in Cuba"
That had just taken San Juan Hill.
Carl Lahser